W9-ANK-385

COMING TO AMERICA

COMING
TO
AMERICA
Immigrants from
SOUTHERN
EUROPE

GLADYS NADLER RIPS

DELACORTE PRESS / NEW YORK

To my parents,
Ethel and Joseph Nadler,
who also came to this country
as immigrants in the second decade of this century.

Published by
Delacorte Press
1 Dag Hammarskjold Plaza
New York, N.Y. 10017

Manufactured in the United States of America
First printing

Picture research by Anne Phalon

Designed by Rhea Braunstein

LIBRARY OF CONGRESS CATALOGING IN PUBLICATION DATA

Rips, Gladys Nadler.
  Coming to America.

  Bibliography: p.
  Includes index.
  SUMMARY: Discusses the experiences of immigrants from Italy, Greece, Portugal, and Spain. Includes a chronology of U.S. immigration laws.
    1. European Americans—History—Juvenile literature. 2. United States—Ethnic relations—Juvenile literature. [1. European Americans—History. 2. United States—Ethnic relations. 3. United States—Emigration and immigration]
  I. Title.
E184.E95R56   973'.04   80-68742
ISBN 0-440-01340-2

Contents

Introduction

Wide open and unguarded stand our gates,
And through them presses a wild, motley throng. . . .
Flying the Old World's poverty and scorn;
These bringing with them unknown gods and rites,
Those, tiger passions, here to stretch their claws.

So wrote poet Thomas Bailey Aldrich in an 1892 issue of the *Atlantic Monthly*. The Statue of Liberty had been unveiled just six years earlier, though Emma Lazarus's lines of poetry, "Give me your tired, your poor . . ." would not be inscribed on the pedestal until 1903. Aldrich's poem represented a rising feeling in America. Too many immigrants were arriving. The "American way of life" was threatened. What had happened in the country where everyone, except the native American Indian and the black slave, was either an immigrant or descended from one?

Before 1880 the vast majority of immigrants had come from northwestern Europe—England, Ireland, Scotland, Wales, Belgium, Denmark, France, Germany, Holland, Norway, Sweden, and Switzerland. After the Civil War, however, immigration from northwest Europe began to slow down. And as Americans became educated, they had less desire to perform the underpaid, unskilled jobs that still needed doing. So immigrants from untapped sources —the countries of southern and eastern Europe— were now sought. Agents from states and private companies fanned out to Italy, Greece, the Austro-Hungarian Empire, Bulgaria, Montenegro, Poland, Rumania, Russia, Serbia, and the Ottoman Empire looking for workers.

And the immigrants came. In 1854 a total of 427,833 arrived; in 1882, 788,992 entered the country. And then came the deluge. The peak year was 1907 when 1,285,349 persons arrived. From 1905 until the start of the First World War in 1914 the million mark was exceeded six times. More immigrants came from 1860 to 1930 than the entire United States population in 1860.

To process such huge numbers the Ellis Island Immigrant Station was opened on January 1, 1892, less than half a mile from the Statue of Liberty in New York Harbor. In the next fifty years some sixteen million immigrants passed through Ellis Island, nearly seventy percent of all those who entered the country. A National Park Service officer said:

To almost everyone who passed through it, and their descendants as well, Ellis Island has been as important in fact as Plymouth Rock has now become in fancy for the descendants of those who came in the first colonization wave.[1]

All steerage passengers on incoming ships had to go to Ellis Island. Before disembarking, all passengers, no matter what class, were inspected on board ship for contagious diseases and for five epidemic diseases: cholera, plague, smallpox, typhus, and yellow fever. Those with suspicious symptoms were taken to Ellis Island.

The arrivals were nervous about their upcoming inspection. In 1911 an observer wrote:

> The immigrants are in a constant turmoil of excitement until they board the ferryboats on the last lap of their journeys. To them Ellis Island is a complicated labyrinth leading to freedom. . . . They obey the signs, gestures and directions of the attendants as dumbly as cattle, and as patiently.[2]

At the height of the immigration tide, signs at Ellis Island were written in nine languages: English, German, Greek, Yiddish, Italian, Hungarian, Polish, Russian, and a Scandinavian (usually Swedish) language. Interpreters stood by to ease the processing. Before he was elected mayor of New York City, Fiorello La Guardia, who knew Italian, German, Yiddish, French, Hungarian, and Croatian, and who himself was the son of Italian immigrants, worked as an interpreter at Ellis Island from 1908 to 1910. He recalled:

> I never managed during the years I worked there to become callous to the mental anguish, the disappointment and the despair I witnessed almost daily. . . . At best the work was an ordeal.[3]

La Guardia and the other interpreters questioned the immigrants as to their destinations and political views near the end of the standard inspection. First they were herded into a mazelike registry room where they awaited their medical exams. The doctors checked for visible physical defects: lameness, blindness, deafness, and the most obvious mental defects. Next came the check for contagious diseases: ringworm, leprosy, venereal diseases, and tuberculosis. Doctors marked with chalk "T.D.," for temporarily detained, on those having suspicious symptoms. Anastasia Stephanios recalls being held at Ellis Island after arriving from Greece because her sister had trachoma, a contagious eye disease:

> I came in 1922. All my family came here: my mother, my sisters, and my brothers. When we came to America, we came to Ellis Island and stayed there two weeks. My brother was in the army. He came to pick us up but couldn't. They said, "You have to stay on Ellis Island two weeks." My youngest sister had something in her eyes. I didn't know what was going to

happen. But the day we could all leave the doctor said, "Your sister can't go out because we have to take her to the hospital." My brother picked us up, but my youngest sister was taken to the hospital. She lived forty days, but after forty days, my sister died.[4]

Fifteen percent of the immigrants at Ellis Island were marked with chalk for further examination. In addition to "T.D.," another major category was "S.I.," special inquiry; usually this was for a suspected criminal or political troublemaker. "L.P.C.," meant likely to become a public charge. Although confusing and anxiety-provoking for immigrants, the system was remarkably efficient. At peak times as many as five thousand people per day were processed through Ellis Island.

Officials at Ellis Island were following laws passed by the federal government. Until 1875 there were no restrictions on the admission of immigrants. But in 1875 Congress responded to the marked antialien feeling in America and excluded criminals and prostitutes. As the result of subsequent acts through 1907, "lunatics," "idiots," "imbeciles," "persons suffering from loathsome and contagious diseases," dependent people, and "subversives" were excluded, as well as those hired as cheap labor by contract from abroad.

Those early laws did not discriminate against any particular nationality, but differences between the "new" immigrants (those arriving after c. 1880) and the "old" immigrants had spurred a new look

xii   *Introduction*

at the laws. By 1910 nearly fifteen percent of the population was foreign-born—not a big increase over the thirteen percent figure for 1860. But their actual numbers were far greater. And their faces, accents, and jobs had changed. From 1821 to 1880 only some two percent of all immigrants came from southern and eastern Europe. From 1901 to 1911 more than seventy percent came from that area which most Americans knew little about. These "new" immigrants tended to live together in big-city ghettos. Would they ever become "real Americans"?

That question was put early and often by many respected members of the national community. Because the Italians were by far the largest nationality among the newer immigrants, the question frequently concerned them. An article in the *Popular Science Monthly* of December 1890 was titled "What Shall We Do with the Dago?" and charged that Italians loved to use their knives "to lop off another dago's finger or ear, or to slash another's cheek."[5] A New York City newspaper in the 1890s wrote:

> The floodgates are open. The bars are down. The sally-ports are unguarded. The dam is washed away. The sewer is choked. Europe is vomiting! In other words, the scum of immigration is viscerating upon our shores. The horde of $9.60 steerage slime is being siphoned upon us from Continental mud tanks.[6]

Prominent New Englanders founded the first Immigration Restriction League in Boston in 1894.

Others sprang up around the country. Labor leaders, who at first had welcomed the new workers, changed their minds. Samuel Gompers, president of the American Federation of Labor and who himself had emigrated from England, argued that "both the intelligence and the prosperity of our working people are endangered by the present immigration. Cheap labor, ignorant labor, takes our jobs and cuts our wages."[7]

John Mitchell, president of the United Mine Workers put it even more forcefully:

> No matter how decent and self-respecting and hard working the aliens who are flooding this country may be, they are invading the land of Americans, and whether they know it or not, are helping to take the bread out of their mouths. America for Americans should be the motto of every citizen, whether he be a working man or a capitalist. . . . There is not enough work for the many millions of unskilled laborers, and there is no need for the added millions who are pressing into our cities and towns to compete with the skilled American in his various trades and occupations. While the majority of the immigrants are not skilled workmen, they rapidly become so, and their competition is not of a stimulating order.[8]

The national clamor almost forced politicians to take a position on the immigration issue. Some, like Senator Henry Cabot Lodge of Massachusetts, joined the anti-Italian crusade with enthusiasm: This

"great Republic should no longer be left unguarded
from them," he said.[9] President Theodore Roosevelt
hoped to cool the controversy by establishing a
commission to study the problem. Known as the
Dillingham Commission, after its chairman Senator
William Paul Dillingham of Vermont, the panel
studied the issue for three years and came out with
a forty-two-volume report. Its conclusions were
heavily weighted against the new immigrants. Serbo-
Croatians had "savage manners"; Poles were "high-
strung"; Italians had "not attained distinguished
success as farmers."

A major goal of restrictionists during this period
was a literacy requirement. Congress first passed
such a law in 1896, but President Grover Cleveland
vetoed it. Congress passed it again in 1913 and
1915 but it was again vetoed, first by William
Howard Taft and then by Woodrow Wilson. Said
Wilson: "Those who come seeking an opportunity
are not to be admitted unless they have already had
one of the chief . . . opportunities they seek, the
opportunity of education."[10] Nonetheless, Congress
passed it two years later in 1917 over his veto.

World War I brought a natural slowdown of
immigration. In fact, Ellis Island was used during
the war to hold prisoners of war and suspected
aliens and spies. Following the war, however, immigration showed signs of reaching new heights. From
June 1920 to June 1921, 805,000 arrived, and more
than sixty-five percent of them were from southern
and eastern Europe. Ellis Island was so jammed that
some ships had to be diverted to Boston.

Antiforeigner sentiment in the country had been raised to a near frenzy by the war, and now more immigrants were heading for America. Congress, responding to pressure, passed its first Quota Act in 1921. It limited new aliens to three percent of each nationality present in the country according to the 1910 census. The 1924 Quota Act went even further, limiting new aliens to two percent of those nationalities present according to the *1890* census —before the new immigrants had arrived in such large numbers.

The law was designed to limit total immigration, but its major goal was to keep out the newer immigrants. The quota from Italy became around 5,000 per year; in 1907, 285,000 Italians had come to America.

Before America moved to close its doors, millions of immigrants had arrived from southern Europe. They would change the composition of the country for good: more than 5 million Italians, 600,000 Greeks, 300,000 Portuguese, and 200,000 Spaniards. What follows is the story of the struggles of those southern Europeans—to leave their native lands, to make a living in the United States, to adjust to the strange new people, attitudes, and customs they met, and to preserve the unique features of their cultures.

FROM ITALY

Chapter 1

Leaving Home

Although individual Italians like Cristoforo Colombo, better known in America as Christopher Columbus, discovered the New World, and Giovanni Caboto, better known as John Cabot, first explored the North American mainland, and Amerigo Vespucci provided America its name, and Giovanni da Verrazzano discovered New York Bay, Italians did not play a major role in the early development of the United States. A small group of Italian glass-makers did settle in America's first successful colony, Jamestown, Virginia, in 1607. "A more damned crew hell never vomited," complained the secretary of the colony.[1] Another group of Italians —two hundred persecuted Protestants—founded New Castle, Delaware, in 1657.

Lorenzo Da Ponte, formerly the librettist for Mozart and himself a dramatist and poet, emigrated to New York in 1805 when he was in his fifties. He became the first professor of Italian literature at

Columbia University and did much to promote Italian culture. At the age of eighty-four he formed an opera company. In his autobiography he described the public reaction to Italian opera:

> Unimaginable the enthusiasm in the cultivated portions of the public aroused by our music when executed by singers of the most perfect taste and highest merit. The *Barbiere di Siviglia* of the universally admired and praised Rossini, was the opera fortunate enough to plant the first root of the great tree of Italian music in New York.[2]

Still, by 1850 only a little more than three thousand Italians lived in all the United States. Americans knew little about Italy and Italians, and Italians, if possible, knew even less about America. Constantine M. Panunzio, who came to Boston in 1902, described in his book, *The Soul of an Immigrant,* his view of America as a young boy in Italy:

> Of course, like every Italian boy, I had heard from earliest childhood of America, the continent which "Colombo," one of our countrymen, had long ago discovered. However . . . to me there was no distinction between North and South America. There was but one America. I had read something of Boston and New York, but the words brought only a vague and indefinite idea to my mind. . . . I had read something of the Indians, who were very much like the cannibals of my childhood stories. [My]

uncle . . . would often recount stories of his voyages to America, but these presented vague pictures and were invariably connected with thrilling experiences with pirates which he had had off the coast of that continent.[3]

The few Italians who had settled in America were generally upper-class, well-educated northern Italians. Those who came in such large numbers after 1880 were generally illiterate peasants (*contadini*), from the southern provinces known as the Mezzogiorno, "the land that time forgot." What caused so many southerners to risk all and leave for the land they knew so little about?

It was not a single event or a sudden change in the lives of the *contadini* that led to the decision to leave. Italy had endured hundreds of years of exploitation under feudal lords and foreign monarchies. But after 1848, ideas of constitutional government were in the air, and Giuseppe Mazzini and the Count di Cavour spoke out for a unified Italy and a representative form of government in a movement called the Risorgimento. Challenges were made against the Austrian Hapsburgs in the north and against the Bourbons in the south, but it took more than a decade of fighting, from 1859 to 1870, and the help of the French, before Giuseppe Garibaldi's forces finally secured all the states of Italy under one rule. Unification, however, did not bring peace to the country, and virtual civil war existed during the 1860s as the southern Italians reacted violently to the high-handed policies of the northerners who had taken over the reins of government.

The south was crushed by massive military force from the north, and there were many executions and other brutal deaths before an uneasy quiet returned to the south. The north was simply ignorant of the south, and major social, economic, and political differences remained. For southerners, who had hoped for quick reforms after unification, the feelings of separation between the peasant believer in popular democratic government and the liberal, wealthy, and well-educated patriots who governed were strong. Reforms were not forthcoming, government bungling and corruption continued with little change except that different people were in charge after 1870. Emigration for many southerners became their only choice.

The new government did nothing to relieve the problems of the agricultural south. No action was taken against the wealthy absentee landlords who charged the peasants high rents and acted much like the overbearing Bourbons, perpetuating the idea that the peasant was condemned forever to misery.[4] It increased the taxes on grain and raised the price of salt, making it nearly impossible for the peasants to store any food. The land itself was in bad shape. Through the centuries it had been deforested. There were no trees to hold back the rain and prevent soil and rocks from washing down the hills. The valleys became malaria-infested swamps. Hot, dry air burned out southern Italy much of the year.

Farmers driven off the land tried to find employment in the industrialized north. The cost of living doubled from 1870 to 1890, causing a decline in the real income of the peasants. Jobs for the growing population became scarce all over Italy. Official reports show that in Naples in 1881 two thirds of the city's population were without work or food.

In addition, southern Italy was struck by unusually harsh natural disasters in the latter half of the nineteenth and the early part of the twentieth centuries. A disease called phylloxera nearly wiped out the vineyards. Mount Vesuvius erupted in 1906, burying whole towns in the province of Naples. Mount Etna in Sicily erupted in 1910. A series of earthquakes hit the provinces of Basilicata and Calabria in 1905. In 1908 a major earthquake and tidal wave struck the Strait of Messina, between Sicily and the mainland. Most of the city of Messina was destroyed and nearly one hundred thousand people died. More than three hundred villages were leveled.

While the situation became increasingly desperate, the impoverished southern peasant farmers heard from relatives and fellow townsmen who had emigrated. Across the ocean was a land in which they could enrich themselves in a relatively short time. To the peasants the family was the center of life. No bond, no allegiance to king or country, could be stronger. To separate, to break up the family even temporarily, was extremely difficult. Conditions in Italy had to be desperate for young men to leave their families behind. Vincent Gianelli explained simply to an interviewer: "The opportunity of finding employment that would be halfway decent wasn't there."⁵ And so the men left, alone.

Hunger was even a more driving force than unemployment. Clarence Silva, who came during the 1920s at the age of nineteen, said:

> We had to live the best way we could. I remember my mother, sometimes she used to go to the city—we lived in a small village— she'd go to the city and buy macaroni and then she'd cook. We used to say: "Come on, Mom, eat." "No, I want to see that you get enough. You have enough, and then I'll get some," she said. We used to fight for survival.⁶

Living conditions were primitive for many of the peasants. Pascal D'Angelo, son of a poor Italian farm worker, left Italy in 1909. In his autobiography, *Son of Italy,* he described his home:

> This garret was divided into two unequal parts. The largest in front where the roof descended very low was filled with firewood. In the small center part was the bed on which my mother, my father, my brother and I slept. A very narrow bed it was. Almost every night I fell, having my head continually decorated with swollen spots about the size of a full ripe cherry. The reason for these falls was my being laid asleep beneath my mother's and father's feet, because I was bigger than my brother and therefore could better guard myself. My brother was two years younger than I. He lay

between them while they slept uncomfortably on either side as if margining the space of his safety. As I slept crosswise beneath their feet they could never stretch their legs, for whenever they did so they felt my little body and immediately shrank back frightened lest they push me off the bed. In spite of my few years, I sometimes could not sleep for lack of sufficient room. But when my parents got up to go to work, I could choose a better place, I and my brother being left on the bed to sleep all we wished.

One night . . . I suddenly awoke with a cry. . . . A heavy patter of down-pouring rain was sweeping the rustic tile roof above our heads. It was the frequent and heavy drops of rain falling on my face that awoke me. . . .

In the lower part of the house was a general living room, kitchen and dining room. At night it was the sleeping place for the animals—the goats and sheep which we were lucky enough to own.[7]

Pascal set out for America with his father, the two hoping to make a lot of money in America and return home in a few years. They were not unusual. Most immigrants planned to return to Italy and lead the good life. Rocco Corresca was an orphan in Italy who came to America almost by chance. He too dreamed of returning to Italy someday:

When I was a very small boy I lived in Italy in a large house with many other small boys,

who were all dressed alike and were taken care
of by some nuns. . . .

They taught us our letters and how to pray
and say the catechism, and we worked in the
fields during the middle of the day. We always
had enough to eat and good beds to sleep in at
night, and sometimes there were feast days,
when we marched about wearing flowers.

Those were good times and they lasted till
I was nearly eight years of age. Then an old
man came and said he was my grandfather. He
showed some papers and cried over me and
said that the money had come at last and now
he could take me to his beautiful home. He
seemed very glad to see me and after they
looked at his papers he took me away and we
went to the big city—Naples. He kept talking
about his beautiful house, but when we got
there it was a dark cellar that he lived in and I
did not like it at all. . . . There were four other
boys in the cellar and the old man said they
were all my brothers. All were larger than I
and they beat me at first till one day Francisco
said they should not beat me anymore, and
then Paulo, who was the largest of all, fought
him till Francisco threw a knife and gave him
a cut. Then Paulo, too, got a knife and said
that he would kill Francisco, but the old man
knocked them both down with a stick and took
their knives away and gave them beatings.

Each morning we boys all went out to beg
and we begged all day near the churches and at

night near the theatres, running to the carriages and opening the doors and then getting in the way of the people so that they had to give us money or walk over us. The old man often watched us and at night he took all the money, except when we could hide something. . . .

Begging was not bad in the summer time because we went all over the streets and there was plenty to see, and if we got much money we could spend some buying things to eat. The old man knew we did that. He used to feel us and smell us to see if we had eaten anything, and he often beat us for eating when we had not eaten.

Early in the morning we had breakfast of black bread rubbed over with garlic or with a herring to give it a flavor. The old man would eat the garlic or the herring himself, but he would rub our bread with it, which he said was as good. He told us that boys should not be greedy and that it was good to fast and that all the saints had fasted. He had a figure of a saint in one corner of the cellar and prayed night and morning that the saint would help him get money. He made us pray, too, for he said that it was good luck to be religious.[8]

Rocco stayed with the old man for three years. When his "grandfather" threatened to make him a cripple so he could earn more money, Rocco decided to run away and talked his friend Francisco into going with him. They worked their way to

America aboard a ship. Ships from southern Italy left from Palermo or Taormina in Sicily, or from Naples on the mainland. Steam power had made it possible to make the crossing in about fifteen days. Steamship companies vied with each other for passengers. The average steerage charge was $30 (raised to $65 in 1915), but price wars among the companies sometimes made it as little as $15 or $16. No matter what the charge, steerage passengers had a rough time. The Dillingham Commission reported in 1911 that steerage

is the poorest possible introduction to, and preparation for, America. It inevitably lowers the standard of decency, even of the immigrants, and too often breaks down their moral and physical stamina. It shatters their bright visions of American life, and lands them cynical and embittered. . . . The ventilation is almost always inadequate, and the air soon becomes foul. The unattended vomit of the seasick, the odors of not too clean bodies, the reek of food and the awful stench of nearby toilet rooms make the atmosphere of the steerage such that it is a marvel that human flesh can endure it. . . . Most immigrants lie in their berths for most of the voyage, in a stupor caused by the foul air. The food often repels them. . . . It is almost impossible to keep personally clean. All of these conditions are naturally aggravated by the crowding.[9]

All steerage quarters were crowded and filthy, but Guido Gallucci, who made the trip with his sister in 1907 to join his parents who were already in America, traveled under most unusual conditions:

> In the middle of the room, where some bunks had been taken away, there was a closed stall about four feet high and in it was a horse! . . . this animal belonged to a rich American who was in first class and this was the only place they could find room for him. All this was very puzzling because most Italian ships have a government representative on board as the law required. There was such a man but he seemed to think it was a great joke, so I guess he must have been paid to allow it.
>
> So the horse was with us while we slept and while we ate. He was a nervous horse, and he stomped a lot and neighed and made funny noises all the time except when it was dark.[10]

Guido Gallucci and millions like him suffered the trip in steerage and entered the country at Ellis Island or other ports.

Chapter 2

Finding Work

Constantine Panunzio was not the typical Italian immigrant, but the situation he found himself in was not unusual. He knew no English, but he had been educated in Italian. Most immigrants knew no English and nearly half of those from southern Italy were illiterate in Italian as well. Constantine had just fifty cents; the average immigrant left Ellis Island with seventeen dollars in his pocket. In nearly every case the immigrant had to find a job and find it fast. Panunzio was on his own.

On his fifth day in America he met and made friends with a French sailor named Louis. They decided to look for a job together and headed for a boardinghouse in the Italian section of Boston, called the North End:

> It was a "three-room apartment" and the land-lady informed us that she was already "full," but since we had no place to go, she would take us in. Added to the host that was already

gathered there, our coming made fourteen people. At night the floor of the kitchen and the dining table were turned into beds. Louis and I were put to sleep in one of the beds with two other men, two facing north and two south. . . .

We began to make inquiries about jobs and were promptly informed that there was plenty of work at "pick and shovel." We were also given to understand by our fellow-boarders that "pick and shovel" was practically the only work available to Italians. Now these were the first two English words I had heard and they possessed great charm. Moreover, if I were to earn money to return home and this was the only work available for Italians, they were very weighty words for me, and I must master them as soon and as well as possible and then set out to find their hidden meaning. I practised for a day or two until I could say "peek" and "shuvle" to perfection. Then I asked a fellow-boarder to take me to see what the work was like. He did. He led me to Washington Street, not far from the colony, where some excavation work was going on, and there I did see, with my own eyes, what the "peek" and "shuvle" were about. My heart sank within me, for I had thought it some form of office work; but I was game and since this was the only work available for Italians, and since I must have money to return home, I would take it up.[1]

In spite of their misgivings, Constantine and Louis headed for North Square, where they had seen other immigrants in search of jobs. Soon they met up with a *padrone,* a labor contractor.

According to a study done in New York in 1897 the padrones controlled about two thirds of the Italian labor in the city. Before 1885 padrones recruited peasants in Italy for work in America. But that year Congress, in an effort to protect immigrants from crooked labor contractors, forbade laborers to come to the United States under contract. The padrones simply shifted the base of their operations to America.

Many padrones took advantage of the immigrants, but they also provided temporary food and lodging and found them work. When they realized they were being cheated, most immigrants would have agreed with one who said:

> We are ignorant and do not know English. Our boss brought us here, knows where to find work, makes contracts with the companies. What should we do without him?[2]

Even if they had known English, immigrants looking for a job on their own would have run into trouble. In 1895 the Croton Reservoir was being built to supply the water needs of New York City. The Help Wanted ad that appeared in newspapers and on handbills read:

> Common labor, white $1.30 to $1.50
> Common labor, colored $1.25 to $1.40
> Common labor, Italian $1.15 to $1.25[3]

Because they were aware it would be difficult to find work in America, many immigrants arranged through relatives or former neighbors to have a padrone meet them at Ellis Island. When Pascal D'Angelo and his father arrived in 1910 a padrone escorted them to Hillsdale, New York, where a number of their former neighbors were at work building roads. Pascal and his father spent five relatively happy years, moving from place to place, building roads with the same gang. The padrone, who worked with them as foreman, was good to them. When family troubles forced the padrone to return to Italy, the gang of eight men went to New York City in search of work. There they met another padrone who told them he had jobs for them all in West Virginia. Each man had to pay a five-dollar "railroad fare" to the padrone. After a terrible trip, during which all their luggage was lost, the gang arrived at camp and went to sleep on some boards covered with dirty straw.

A fatal accident soon killed two members of Pascal's gang, and the group that was left quit and returned to New York. Shortly afterward Pascal's father decided to return to Italy:

> "We are not better off than when we started," he said, and asked me if I wished to go back with him.
>
> I shook my head. Something had grown in me during my stay in America. Something was keeping me in this wonderful perilous land where I had suffered so much and where I had

so much more to suffer. Should I quit this great America without a chance to really know it? Again I shook my head. There was a lingering suspicion that somewhere in this vast country an opening existed, that somewhere I would strike the light. I could not remain in the darkness perpetually.[4]

Bad as Pascal's experience was, at least he was permitted to leave the work camp and try to pursue his dream of America. There were many reports of camps where Italian laborers were held as slaves. Some were even shot by guards as they tried to escape. A laborer in the 1890s recounts his experience:

We started from New York in November 3, 1891, under the guidance of two bosses. We had been told we should go to Connecticut to work on a railroad and earn one dollar and seventy-five cents per day. We were taken instead to South Carolina, first to a place called Lambs and then after a month or so to the "Tom Tom" sulphate mines. The railroad fare was eight dollars and eighty-five cents; this sum, as well as the price of our tools, nearly three dollars, we owed to the bosses. We were received by an armed guard, which kept constant watch over us, accompanying us every morning from the barracks to the mines and at night again from the work to our shanty. . . . Part of our pay went toward the extinction of our debt; the rest was spent for as much food as we could get at the "pluck-me" store. We got only so much as would keep us from starvation. Things cost us more than twice or three times their regular price. Our daily fare was coffee and bread for breakfast, rice with lard or soup at dinner-time, and cheese or sausage for supper. Yet we were not able to pay off our debt; so after a while we were given only bread, and with this only to sustain us we had to go through our daily work. By and by we became exhausted, and some of us got sick. Then we decided to try, at the risk of our lives, to escape. Some of us ran away, eluding the guards. After a run of an hour I was exhausted and decided to stay for the night in the woods. We were, however, soon surprised by the appearance of the bosses and two guards. They thrust guns in our faces and ordered us to return to work or they would shoot us down. We answered that we would rather die than resume our former life in the mine. The bosses then sent for two black policemen, who insisted that we should follow them. We went before a judge, who was sitting in a barroom. The judge asked if there was any written contract, and when he heard that there wasn't, said he would let us go free. But the bosses, the policemen, and the judge then held a short consultation, and the result was that the bosses paid some money (I believe it was forty-five dollars), the policemen put the manacles on our wrists, and we were marched off. At last, on April 1, we

were all dismissed on account of the hot
weather. My comrades took the train for New
York. I had only one dollar, and with this, not
knowing either the country or the language, I
had to walk to New York. After forty-two days
I arrived in the city utterly exhausted. . . .[5]

Eighty percent of the immigrants from Italy during this period were male, from southern Italy, and
between the ages of fourteen and forty-five—working age. They settled in the northeastern United
States. So many had bad experiences that more than
a third of those who arrived in the 1880s and 1890s
returned to Italy. Those who stayed, however,
accomplished a great deal. Most of them stuck at
jobs that involved heavy, unskilled labor. The pick
and shovel became the symbol of the Italian worker.
They helped to build the nation's railroads, dig the
subways (more than four thousand toiled in the
New York underground system), pave the roads,
fell the trees, load and unload the freight, and dig
the mines.

Constantine Panunzio had many different jobs
after arriving in America. His first pick and shovel
job proved to be the standard situation of bad
working conditions and brutal padrones. He and
Louis left it after three days.

They managed to get back to Boston and find a
place to sleep in the filthy boardinghouse they had
roomed in before. Soon they signed on for a job at
a lumbering camp in Maine. Constantine had never
wielded an axe and proved to be not very good at

it. He and Louis took off, again without pay. A short stint in a factory followed. That did not work out because the other workers, mostly Russian immigrants, resented the "foreigners." He and Louis found work in another logging camp, manned primarily by French Canadians. Louis felt at home with the French Canadians and decided to stay. Constantine was fired because he still could not chop down a tree. He next found work with a farmer named George Annis, in Stacyville, Maine, who agreed to pay him fifteen dollars a month, with room and board:

> I worked on George Annis' farm until late fall, and in the winter I went into the woods with him and worked as "cookie" or assistant cook, in a lumbering camp of his own. In the early spring we returned to the farm. The time had at last come when I was ready to return to Italy. I had worked for six months: at $15 per month that meant $90. I had received only five dollars in cash, and that would leave $85 coming to me, which would certainly be sufficient to buy me a third class passage and leave something with which to purchase a few gifts to take back with me. . . . About the first of the month I went to Mr. Annis and asked him to pay me. He said he would do so in a few days. The middle of the month was now approaching and the time for my departure was near, so again I went to him. It was then that the truth came out. He laughed me out of

court and with a sneer upon his lips which I
remember to this very day, he handed me a
five-dollar bill and said that that was all he
could pay me.[6]

Constantine was so mad at Annis he decided to
go to Boston and ask the Italian lawyer there to
help him get the money he was owed. Five dollars
was not enough for the train fare, but a friend
advised Constantine to hop on the coal tender of a
passing train and ride for free. When the train
stopped at a small town in Vermont, he was
awakened by a man shaking his shoulder:

"You stay in this town tonight. Come with me
and I'll put you up." . . . I was really thankful
for his offer of shelter and thought to myself
that after all Americans *were* kind to traveling
strangers, as we were in Italy.

The big man took hold of my hand and led
me through the dark streets. . . . We came to
a narrow alley, which seemed darker than ever.
The big man pulled a key from his pocket and
opened a door. He led me in, still holding me
by the hand, and locked the door within. Then
he lighted a small kerosene lamp, and I looked
around. I said to myself, "What a funny sort of
house this man lives in; he must be a hermit."
It was a square room, with walls of bare bricks.
There was no picture on the walls and not a
sign of human habitation. To the right were
two tiny rooms, more like small alcoves; in
each was a small bunk-like arrangement with

straw spread upon it. He pointed to one of
these and said, "You can sleep there for now."
Then he began to move toward the door, while
I looked at him in amazement. As he
approached the door, still with his back to it,
he took out the key and unlocked it with his
hand behind him, still facing me. I reached for
the lamp, which was on a little shelf in the
alcove, thinking to give him more light. As I
reached for it, he slipped out with a quick
movement and turned the key from the outside.
Then I saw the bars in the windows. With this
the awful realization came over me: I was in
jail.[7]

A kind judge listened to Constantine's story and
imposed no punishment; he sent Constantine back
to Stacyville. There, he found that Annis had dis-
appeared and a man named John Carter had taken
over the farm.

Maine was a "dry" state in which the sale of
liquor was illegal. Carter soon began using Constantine to order the liquor for him elsewhere. Slowly,
Constantine came to realize the reason for all the
secrecy. It was brought home to him the night of a
fair when he was nearly caught by the sheriff selling
bottles of liquor to lumbermen. His second brush
with the law upset him a great deal:

Life was now becoming hopeless in the extreme. I began to suspect every one with whom
I came in contact and to doubt whether there
was such a thing as right or justice. Here I had

worked for nearly a year in an attempt to earn sixty or seventy dollars to return home, and I had been deceived at every turn, and those whom I trusted had proved to be traitors. I had made sacrifices; I had been subjected to humiliation, to reach a worthy goal, only to be taken advantage of, only to find myself penniless, and what was infinitely worse, to be forced into a life of lawlessness.[8]

But he did not give up. He did leave Carter and soon was hired by another farmer and, as Constantine put it, "at last I found myself in a genuine American home."[9]

Constantine Panunzio got his real start in America on a farm. Most immigrants stayed in large cities, struggling to survive. An amazing number managed to become successful, adding to the American dream.

Before they left Italy, many emigrants believed the streets in America were paved with gold. When they arrived, one immigrant related, they discovered the streets were not paved with gold; the streets were not even paved—*they* were going to have to pave them. But for millions of illiterate, unskilled workers the vision of gold in America became reality.

Chapter 3

New Horizons

Not all Italian immigrants remained in the major cities of the northeast or sought work as common laborers. In fact, immigration officials in America and in Italy urged immigrants to head for the countryside. Bruno Roselli, an Italian journalist, put it this way:

> You are unsuccessful and unhappy here. You cannot compete in business with the Jew, while your ignorance of English puts you at a disadvantage with the Irishman. Get away from such competition, and let us see whether your strong arms will not bring abundant riches out of the soil. . . . You . . . lacked opportunities in Europe and [will fail] to find them here when in cities crowded with craftier peoples, but [may thrive] when facing the obstacles of nature.[1]

Some remarkable success stories of earlier immigrants inspired those who came later. Amedeo Obici, born in the province of Treviso in 1877, came to the United States when he was twelve. He went to live with his uncle in Scranton, Pennsylvania, and was enrolled in school the following week. Working for fruit vendors, cigar makers, and a café owner, Amedeo earned enough money to send for his mother and two sisters. He decided it was time to go into business for himself. He rented space outside a store, borrowed money to build a stand, and began selling fresh roasted peanuts.

Amedeo increased his business by putting coupons bearing the letters of his name inside the five-cent bags of shelled peanuts, one letter per package. Those who spelled out his name with the coupons received a watch that cost a dollar. He gave away twenty thousand watches in two years. In 1906, less than ten years after he had begun, Amedeo incorporated the Planters Peanut Company of Wilkes-Barre, Pennsylvania. By 1931 he was doing more than twelve million dollars in business annually.

Even as Obici was making his fortune in Pennsylvania, California was viewed as the true land of opportunity by Italian immigrants with the strength, ambition, and resources to get there. In fact, largely because of the climate, California was known to many as "Italy in America." By 1897 there were over forty-five thousand Italians in California, and just three years later fifteen thousand more had arrived. By 1920 Italians made up nearly twelve percent of California's foreign stock, the largest foreign population in the state. Most were living in and around the San Franciso area, and many became wealthy.

Andrea Sbarboro came to the United States in 1852 from Genoa. By 1875 he was a banker interested in investing some of his money in the land. In 1881 he set up his Italian-Swiss Agricultural Colony about a hundred miles north of San Francisco. He named his town Asti—after a town in Italy—and hired immigrants to work the land. He tried to convince the workers to buy stock in his business, to become part owners. The workers, however, were more interested in getting their full salary of $30 to $40 a month and rejected his offer. At first it seemed they had made a wise decision. Sbarboro's product was table grapes, and by the time his first crop was ready, the market price had fallen from $30 a ton to $8. He decided to switch to wine making in a desperate effort to save his business. He hired Pietro Rossi as chief wine maker and by 1890 the colony was a success. Stock worth $135,000 when it was issued in 1880 was worth more than $3 million in 1910. Sbarboro himself described his accomplishments in a 1900 magazine article:

> In less than twenty years the colonists have changed the sheep-ranch into a beautiful vineyard of two thousand acres, erected one of the largest wineries in the State, built a settlement for one hundred families, erected a school-

house where many children, most of them born on the premises, already attend, have a railroad station, post-office, and telephone, and have laid the foundation for a new city.[2]

Other Italians established million-dollar agricultural businesses in California. Perhaps the most famous are Marco J. Fontana and Antonio Ceruti, who started a canning company under the name Marca del Monte ("brand of the mountain"), which was later shortened to Del Monte.

As farmers and fishermen began to make money in northern California, they wanted to bank it in Italian savings and loan associations. There were quite a number of these by the turn of the century; Sbarboro alone had founded six. But the most famous Italian banker by far was Amadeo Pietro Giannini, the son of Genoese immigrants.

Giannini sensed the need for a bank that poor Italian immigrants could use to deposit their savings in and borrow capital from to get started in business. He opened his bank in 1904 in the North Beach Italian immigrant section of San Francisco and called it the Bank of Italy. Small stockholders—grocers, produce handlers, bakers, cobblers—had purchased over half the shares. The San Francisco banking community laughed at Giannini's operation and called it "that little dago bank in North Beach."

They were not laughing for long. When the earthquake hit San Francisco in 1906, Giannini and some friends managed to get to his bank before fires consumed it and remove all his gold reserves and bank records in orange crates. Four days after the earthquake, while the rest of the city still smoldered, Giannini opened for business. From that point on the Bank of Italy grew more and more successful, but Giannini always stressed the importance of the small investor. He was the first to establish branch banks in California. By 1930 he controlled thirty percent of the California banking business. By 1948 Giannini's bank—known now as the Bank of America—was the largest in the country. Today it is the largest in the world. Giannini attributed his success to hard work:

> Too many people waste time in useless ways. I was never interested in the local gossips or scandals, nor in anything whatsoever foreign to my business. When you have a clear-cut object . . . don't dawdle. My method is concentration. I have always avoided loading my mind and memory with useless stuff. I don't try to keep track of baseball records or golf championships or the late developments in any activity not connected with the banking business.[3]

Millionaires were, of course, the exception that fueled the dreams of immigrants. And perhaps their success inspired those who sought different opportunities in the United States. Although many immigrants had been farmers in Italy, few had the money or the inclination to try it in America. Italian farms were small and close together; the sense of community was terribly important to the peasant. The

wide open spaces in the Midwest did not appeal to
the immigrant, even if he had had the money to
purchase the land. Consequently, the immigrants
who tried farming usually did it either on a small
scale—a few acres, a truck farm—or cooperatively.

Italian-American truck farms flourished (and
many still exist) in the New York Finger Lakes
region, Long Island, Staten Island, around New
Haven, in Delaware, and in southern New Jersey.
Small farm communities sprang up in the South—
Texas, Arkansas, Mississippi, Alabama, Tennessee,
Virginia, and particularly, Louisiana. A 1904 news-
paper article by one C. L. Buck of Independence,
Louisiana, explained:

> The majority of farmers here have done away
> with negro labor. Why? Because they are a
> shiftless, worthless sort, whereas the Italian
> laborer is a success. His sole object is to make
> money, and he knows it must come out of the
> ground; therefore, he is always at work when
> his work is needed.
>
> They are prompt to pay their debts at the
> stores, meet their paper at the banks when
> due, and often before. . . . I find it a great
> improvement and cheaper than the negro labor
> of today.[4]

Sunnyside, in Arkansas, was one of the first
attempts to establish an agricultural cooperative in
the South. Austin Corbin, who owned the Long
Island Railroad, imported five hundred immigrant
families directly from Rome. Most knew no English;

many had never been on a farm; none had ever farmed cotton. In addition, Sunnyside was never well drained and was full of mosquitoes. In 1896, 130 people died of malaria in two months, mostly women and children. The next year a majority of the Italians fled in panic. In the autumn of 1899 malaria struck again and 80 colonists died within one month. The death of Corbin, who planned to drain the land and set up health facilities, doomed the colony.

A Catholic priest, Father Pietro Bandini, newly arrived in America to help Italian immigrants, appeared in Arkansas about this time and offered to help the few remaining families. Father Bandini made arrangements for the colonists to move to spots in Missouri and Arkansas. He made a shrewd bargain with the St. Louis and San Francisco Railroad, getting them to sell nine hundred acres in the northwest corner of Arkansas to the immigrants for just a dollar an acre. He even got Queen Margherita of Italy to send money to build a church. The colonists managed to survive a cyclone the first year, and within a few years they were enjoying some success dairying, grape growing, and fruit raising. They named the new community Tontitown in honor of Enrico Tonti, the Italian who had explored Arkansas with the French explorer La Salle in the seventeenth century. Their troubles were not over, however. Local residents resented the presence of the immigrants and twice burned the community's church to the ground. When a mob approached for the third time, Father Bandini said:

We are all Americans here and I give you
notice that we shall exercise the American
right of self-defense. There are few men among
us who have not served in the Italian army. We
are familiar with our guns. I am hereafter
colonel of our regiment and I assure you that
night and day a sentinel shall patrol our streets.
Any person coming among us and manifesting
malice will be shot.[5]

Bandini's strong stance scared off the mob, and
there was no more trouble from local residents.
Tontitown remains today a successful agricultural
community, with canning factories and marketing
facilities nearby. Its success, and others, prompted
the Dillingham Commission to conclude:

The rural community has had a salutary effect
on the Italians, especially those from the
southern provinces. . . . In many cases it has
taken an ignorant, unskilled, dependent foreign
laborer and made of him a shrewd self-
respecting independent farmer and citizen.[6]

Prejudice always leads to misunderstandings and
often to violence, as it did at Tontitown. Unfor-
tunately, the incident at Tontitown was not an isolated one. The most horrifying case involving Italian
immigrants occurred in New Orleans, Louisiana, in
1891.
    Italians—particularly Sicilians—had done very
well in Louisiana as fishermen and truck farmers.
By 1850 Louisiana had more Italians than any other

state and as late as 1910 New Orleans had a higher proportion of Italian immigrants than any other city. As they did practically everywhere, the Italians worked, lived, and socialized together. Rumors flew about a Sicilian-based crime ring called the Mafia. When the New Orleans police chief was killed during an investigation into the Mafia's activities, hundreds of Italians were rounded up for questioning. Nine were tried for the crime. Six were acquitted and a mistrial was declared for the other three. Two days later the leading citizens of New Orleans led a mob of six thousand to eight thousand and stormed the jail. Ten Italians were shot to death and it was decided to take a man named Polize, who was only wounded, outside to be executed. The mob wanted a public hanging. On March 15, 1891, *The New York Times* reported what happened:

> Polize, the crazy man, was locked up in a cell upstairs. The doors were flung open and one of the avengers, taking aim, shot him through the body. He was not killed outright and in order to satisfy the people on the outside, who were crazy to know what was going on within, he was dragged down the stairs and through the doorway by which the crowd had entered. A rope was provided and tied around his neck and the people pulled him up to the crossbars. Not satisfied that he was dead, a score of men took aim and poured a volley of shot into him, and for several hours the body was left dangling in the air.[7]

Congratulatory messages from across the country poured in for the leaders of the mob, and protests by Italian-American groups in New York and other major cities were largely ignored.

The New Orleans inquiry—and resulting massacre—was the first publicized investigation into the activities of the Mafia, but it was by no means the last. The Kefauver Senate Crime Investigating Committee described the Mafia in 1951 as a "nationwide crime syndicate" controlling the most lucrative rackets in American cities. The Mafia is reputed to have had its origin centuries ago in Sicily as an association to protect the poor and the helpless against the excessive power of the Church, the police, and the rich. As time went on, the organization turned from helping the poor peasants to exploiting them. Not above duping and robbing the Church, the Mafia was also adept at bribing officials and electing and manipulating politicians. Its weapons were often fear, extortion, and the knife.

Characterized by secrecy, strange rituals, and organization in families of strictly Italian origin, the Mafia reportedly came to the United States in the 1880s and continued its activities with an American flavor. During the Prohibition era in the 1920s and 1930s, for example, millions of dollars were made by racketeers from selling illegal liquor and "protection." "Murder Incorporated" caused hundreds of people to be shot and killed by their "hit men" for nonpayment, revenge, or infringement of the rules. In 1936, a young prosecutor from New York, Thomas E. Dewey, who later ran unsuccessfully for president of the United States, finally cracked down on the rackets and sent many mobsters to jail, many of whom were indeed Italian in origin. The criminals themselves denied the existence of the Mafia, and Italian-Americans protested once again the slur against their good name.

The arrest of sixty known racketeers from all over the United States at a secret meeting in Apalachin, New York, in 1957 brought no convictions, but indicated clearly the national scope of the underworld. The testimony in 1963 of convicted murderer Joseph Valachi from prison painted a vivid and detailed picture of the organization he called Cosa Nostra, "Our Thing," leaving little further doubt about the existence of the Mafia. The recent popularity of Mario Puzo's novel *The Godfather* attests to the acceptance by most people of the Mafia as both legend and fact today.

Nonetheless, just as the violence of those early days in New Orleans must be deplored, so must the notion of a connection between the Mafia and all Italian-Americans be contradicted today. The Mafia is only part of the story of millions of Italians who came to the United States. And the beginnings of such desperately vicious and sinister activities attributed to the Mafia may someday well be explained at least in part by the conditions in American cities at the turn of the century.

After the Civil War "Little Italys" mushroomed in all the major cities of the northeast, with New York City the favorite of Italian immigrants.

The New York Little Italy appeared to an outsider as nothing more than a sprawling slum. The housing consisted of dingy, overcrowded, unheated tenements, many of which lacked inside toilets. As many as fourteen people would live in a three-room apartment, with four sleeping in one bed. People would share an apartment or try to find housing in the same building with others who came from the same town in Italy. Families with children would rent rooms to single men in order to help pay the rent. Jacob Riis, an immigrant from Denmark, worked as a journalist-photographer in New York around the turn of the century and wrote his first impressions of conditions in Little Italy:

> Here is a "flat" of "parlor" and two pitch-dark coops called bedrooms. Truly, the bed is all there is room for. The family tea-kettle is on the stove, doing duty for the time being as a wash-boiler. By night it will have returned to its proper use again, a practical illustration of how poverty . . . makes both ends meet. One, two, three beds are there, if the old boxes and heaps of foul straw can be called by that name; a broken stove with crazy pipe from which the smoke leaks at every joint, a table of rough boards propped up on boxes, piles of rubbish in the corner. The closeness and smell are appalling. How many people sleep here? The woman with the red bandanna shakes her head sullenly, but the bare-legged girl with the bright face counts on her fingers—five, six!

"Six, sir!" Six grown people and five children.[8]

Another tenement in the Mulberry Street section of New York inspected by Riis was in no better shape:

> In a room not thirteen feet either way slept twelve men and women, two or three in bunks set in a sort of alcove, the rest on the floor. A kerosene lamp burned dimly in the fearful atmosphere, probably to guide other and later arrivals to their "beds," for it was only just past midnight. A baby's fretful wail came from an adjoining hall-room, where, in the semi-darkness, three . . . figures could be made out. The "apartment" was one of three in two adjoining buildings we had found, within half an hour, similarly crowded. Most of the men were lodgers, who slept there for five cents a spot.[9]

The experience of an Italian immigrant woman matched those of Jacob Riis:

> We had a sink in the hall with nothing else, and four families to share it. And one bathroom in the yard where garbage was also thrown. How could a body wash and have a bit of privacy that way? I died a little every time I went there.[10]

The New York Little Italy was bigger (population about 350,000 in 1910) than, but not worse than, the Little Italys in other major cities. Constantine Panunzio returned to Boston after twelve years and was startled by the conditions he found there:

> For one thing, here was a congestion the like of which I had never seen before. Within the narrow limits of one-half square mile were crowded together thirty-five thousand people, living tier upon tier, huddled together until the very heavens seemed to be shut out. These narrow alley-like streets of Old Boston were one mass of litter. The air was laden with soot and dirt. Ill odors arose from every direction. Here was no trees; no parks worthy of the name; no playgrounds other than the dirty streets for the children to play on; no birds to sing their songs; no flowers to waft their perfume; and only small strips of sky to be seen; while around the entire neighborhood like a mighty cordon, a thousand thousand wheels of commercial activity whirled incessantly day and night, making noises which would rack the sturdiest of nerves.[11]

Panunzio concluded that "this community, by the will of the American people and that of the immigrants, or more correctly speaking, in the absence of the constructive will of any one group of people, was leading a life almost completely separated from the life of America."[12]

Newly arrived Italians wanted to stay close to family and friends. This, in turn, led to discrimination by the native population, who viewed the

Italians as unwilling to become "Americanized." This led to a stronger sense of community among Italians. For instance, the immigrants tended to settle disputes among themselves, rather than turning to the police, whom they regarded as unfair. But outsiders simply concluded that Italians had no respect for the law.

Since immigrants did not feel part of American celebrations, they had their own. Feast days were a time for all to forget their grim situation and enjoy what they remembered of their native culture. Jacob Riis observed a San Donato's feast day in New York in 1899:

> All the sheets of the tenement had been stretched so as to cover the ugly sheds and outhouses. Against the dark rear tenement the shrine of the saint had been erected, shutting it altogether out of sight with a wealth of scarlet and gold. Great candles and little ones, painted and beribboned, burned in a luminous grove before the altar. The sun shone down upon a mass of holiday-clad men and women, to whom it was all as a memory of home, of the beloved home across the seas. . . . The fire-escapes of the tenement had, with the aid of some cheap muslin draperies, a little tinsel, and the strange artistic genius of this people, been transformed into beautiful balconies, upon which the tenants of the front house had reserved seats. In a corner of the yard over by the hydrant, a sheep, which was to be raffled

off as the climax of the celebration, munched
its wisp of hay patiently, while bare-legged
children climbed its back and pulled its wool.
From the second story of the adjoining house,
which was a stable, a big white horse stuck his
head at intervals out of the window, and sur-
veyed the shrine and the people with an interested look.

The musicians . . . blew "Santa Lucia" on
their horns. The sweetly seductive melody
woke the echoes of the block and its slumber-
ing memories. The old women rocked in their
seats, their faces buried in their hands. The
crowd from the street increased, and the chief
celebrant, who turned out to be no less a person
than the saloon-keeper himself, reaped a liberal
harvest of silver half-dollars. The villagers
bowed and crossed themselves before the saint,
and put into the plate their share toward the
expenses of the celebration.[13]

Riis went on:

San Donato's feast-day is one of very many
such days that are celebrated in New York in
the summer months. By what magic the
calendar of Italian saints was arranged so as
to bring so many birthdays within the season
of American sunshine I do not know. But it is
well.[14]

Certainly today everyone would agree with Riis's
conclusion that it was "well" for Italians to be

holding their own special celebrations. But many Americans at the turn of the century viewed such ceremonies with distrust. It was another instance of Italians being unwilling to take part in the American way of life—and that made many suspicious of them. In spite of the successful businessmen like Obici and Giannini and flourishing agricultural communities like Tontitown, these "new" immigrants would not be fully accepted until they became "Americanized." Many Italian immigrants feared that process, and fought it, for they had no way of predicting how their lives would change as a result.

Chapter 4

Settling In

The first American institution most immigrant families met was the public school system, and more often than not the meeting was painful. Southern Italians valued the family above all else, and the schools represented a threat to this. Constantine Panunzio reported:

> A woman in our constituency had three children, two boys, one seven and the other five years old, and a baby girl. She was a widow and was having a bitter struggle to eke out an existence. She came to me one day requesting that I interest myself in placing the little girl in a nursery, and the boys in a kindergarten or school. I proceeded to make such arrangements at the public school, when one day she came to my office and broke out crying. I could not make out what the trouble was. After she calmed down, I asked her to tell me the diffi-

culty. After evading several questions, she finally said: "Please don't send my children to an *American school,* for as soon as they learn English they will not be my children anymore. I know many children who as soon as they learn English become estranged from their parents. I want to send my babies to a school where they can be taught in the Italian language." Here, then, is at least one reason why it is possible for many schools, other than public schools, to exist in America, where languages other than English are used almost exclusively. And even though we stifle our emotions as we see a mother plead for the privilege of keeping her children always hers, we still must consider how we can manage to bring them into a knowledge and appropriation of American life and thought in the face of such an attitude.[1]

Learning the language is an obvious reason for attending school, but some immigrants saw no reason to learn English. Poor immigrant families had another reason for resisting sending their sons and daughters to school: Children in school were not working and contributing to the family income. Education for girls was viewed as even less useful than education for boys:

Boys had always more privileges than girls and so the idea of their going to school instead of helping us (parents) was only half bad. Boys somehow managed to make a penny or two, and in this way kept peace with my husband. . . . But when girls at thirteen and fourteen wasted good time in school, it simply made us regret our coming to America.[2]

A favorite expression of southern Italians was *Una mazza, lavoro e pane fanno i figli belli* ("A cane, work, and bread make for fine children"). Nevertheless, after they had decided to remain in America, southern Italians sent their children to school in the same percentages as other immigrant groups. The children were exposed to a new world, and this did have an effect on family life. The child's struggle to become Americanized, to feel a part of his or her group at school, often led to misunderstandings at home, creating a gap between parent and child. Angelo Pellegrini, who came to America in 1913 and settled in McCleary, Washington, related the following incident in his autobiography:

One day in hygiene class we were discussing the care of the teeth. This led quite naturally to an appraisal of the sets of teeth in the classroom. Everyone talked glibly of visits to the dentist, of a certain number of cavities filled, of the excruciating pain bravely endured in the dentist's chair, etc. What did Angelo have to report? Nothing. Absolutely nothing. I had never heard of a dentist up to that day. . . . I felt very much embarrassed—an alien, an inferior breed who had never had what everybody could boast of: a tooth cavity drilled and filled by a dentist.

For a brief while I felt like an oddity. And then, quite unexpectedly, I became a hero. The teacher asked me if I would let her look at my teeth. . . . When she had completed the examination she announced to the class with considerable and undisguised excitement that she had seen a miracle: a perfect set of teeth.[3]

Constantine Panunzio had no family conflicts about education because he had no parents in the United States. But when he decided he wanted an education, his first day proved a disaster:

It was about six years since I had left school in Italy. Now I returned to it of my own volition. But soon both Miss Richmond and I discovered that there were other factors to be considered than my willingness to go to school and her desire to teach me. The school, of course, was held in the usual one-roomed schoolhouse so common in the country districts. What happened on that first and second day the reader can easily imagine. Here was a young man twenty years of age sitting in the midst of children ranging from six to fourteen. Not only this, but he knew very little English and had been away from school so long he hardly knew how to handle a book. The test was too great for human nature. The children immediately began to poke fun at the new pupil, to call him names, to throw paper wads at him and torment him in every way, until neither Miss Richmond nor I had a moment of peace the whole day long. It was clear from the very first that it was an impossible situation. I stood it for about a week, then Miss Richmond suggested that I take private lessons at home, to which I gladly consented.[4]

Through the family he was working for, Panunzio managed to get a scholarship to a private high school where the students were closer to his own age. Being the only Italian at the school, he ran into some prejudice, even from the teachers:

"In this country," he [the teacher] said, "it is not customary to carry knives." . . . As he proceeded with words of counsel and admonition, he used the word "stiletto" synonymously with the word "knife." There appeared to be some uncertainty in his mind as to just what it was but one thing was certain: I had a weapon and I was an Italian. That was enough. All Italians carry weapons and are dangerous creatures, according to the common American belief. He assured me that he harbored no ill feelings toward me, but he made it plain that it was not a good thing to carry a weapon and that since coming to the school I had caused great disturbance by openly carrying a "stiletto." . . . "Unless you give it up," he continued, "you will be obliged to leave school."

Finally, . . . to clinch the matter, [he] said that he himself had seen it a few moments before, and for that reason he asked me to remain. If I did not mind, he would at least like to look at it. The point of it was even then to be seen sticking out of my vest pocket, shining brightly against a blue silk handkerchief. I could deny it no longer. Taking hold of the lapel of my coat, he pulled it open, reached for the dreaded weapon and pulled it out. . . .

It was an *aluminum comb,* conveniently pointed at one end to be used for manicuring, and not for carving out human hearts! It did look very much like a stiletto. . . . So far as I know, no explanation was ever made of the matter, and to this day, I venture to say, some of my schoolmates still remember the dreadful days when they went to school with an Italian who carried a stiletto with which he intended to carve out hearts, both men's and maidens'![5]

Panunzio saw the humor of situations like these and continued with his schooling. After graduating from the private school, he went on to Wesleyan University and was graduated. For him, and thousands of other immigrants, education was necessary to make him feel part of his adopted land.

It was not school but the labor unions that were the first American institution to confront many adult immigrants. Southern Italians were skeptical about unions at first. Security had come from family and friends in their old villages. *Chi gioca solo non perde mai* is an ancient Sicilian maxim: "The man who plays a lone hand never loses." Most believed they would only be in the country a short time and did not want to risk losing wages in a strike. Most were obligated to padrones who steered clear of the unions. Union members saw the huge number of Italian laborers as competition for their jobs; they made no effort to recruit the new arrivals and in many cases denied membership to those who sought it. It is not surprising, therefore, that before the turn of the century padrone-controlled Italian immigrants sometimes acted as scabs and strikebreakers. They helped to defeat a longshoremen's strike in 1887 and a Chicago meat-packers' strike in 1904.

That period in American history was one of great unrest among laborers. Public sentiment overwhelmingly favored the owners against the workers. All union agitators were thought to be anarchists really working for the overthrow of the government. Gradually, after years of long hours and low pay, Italian workers began to respond to the arguments of labor leaders—especially the radicals, because they were often the only ones who would have anything to do with Italians.

Italians led a major strike for the first time in 1912—at a textile mill in Lawrence, Massachusetts. The bitter strike lasted for nine weeks, and one of the leaders was Arturo Giovannitti, an official of the radical International Workers of the World (IWW). Early in the strike an Italian woman was killed. Even though Giovannitti had been far from the scene, as the leader of the strike he was charged with murder. If he were found guilty, Giovannitti might be sentenced to the electric chair. In his address to the court he said:

> Weigh both sides and then judge. And if it be, gentlemen of the jury, that your judgement shall be that this gate will be opened and we shall pass out of it and go back into the sunlit world, then let me assure you of what you are doing. Let me tell you that the first strike that breaks out again in this Commonwealth or any other place in America where the word and the help and the intelligence of . . . Arturo Giovannitti will be needed and necessary, there we shall go again regardless of any fear and of any threat.
>
> We shall return again to our humble efforts, obscure, humble, unknown, misunderstood— soldiers of this mighty army of the working class of the world, which out of the shadows and the darkness of the past is striving towards the destined goal which is the emancipation of human kind, which is the establishment of love and brotherhood and justice for every man and woman in this earth.
>
> On the other hand, if your verdict shall be the contrary . . . if it be that these hearts of ours must be stilled on the same death chair and by the same current of fire that has destroyed the life of the wife murderer . . . then I say, gentlemen of the jury, that tomorrow we shall pass into a greater judg-

ment, that tomorrow we shall go from your presence into a presence where history shall give its last word to us.[6]

Giovannitti was acquitted. Some ten years later, Fred C. Moore, one of his lawyers, was again the defense lawyer for Italian immigrants accused of murder—Nicola Sacco and Bartolomeo Vanzetti.

The Sacco-Vanzetti trial in 1921 took place in the years just following the Russian Revolution and World War I in an atmosphere of semihysteria against foreigners and anarchists, who were often assumed to be one and the same. On flimsy circumstantial evidence they were accused of having killed the paymaster and a guard during a 1920 holdup at a shoe factory in South Braintree, Massachusetts. At their trial the defendants' Italian background and radical political opinions were constantly attacked by the prosecution and sneered at by the judge. "I am suffering because I am a radical," Vanzetti said to the jury during his final statement, "and indeed I am a radical. I have suffered because I was an Italian, and indeed I am an Italian."[7] The two were found guilty and sentenced to be electrocuted. After six years of appeals and public protests they were executed in 1927. Vanzetti's last statement asserted his innocence:

I have suffered more for my family and for my beloved than for myself; but I am so convinced to be right that if you could execute me two times, and I could be reborn two other times, I

would live again to do what I have done
already.[8]

Years later, after sifting through the evidence,
historians have been unable to decide whether Sacco
and Vanzetti were guilty or innocent. But there is no
question that at the time they were found guilty
they were convicted because they were radicals and
because they were Italian.

At the same time, the son of an Italian immigrant
father was beginning to show how the political
system could work for the little man. Fiorello La
Guardia had been elected a representative to
Congress from New York City and was rapidly
making a name for himself as an astute politician.
He later introduced legislation in Congress that gave
working people everywhere the right to strike. A
Republican, he was defeated in the Democratic
landslide of 1932 but went on to become the mayor
of New York. His presence encouraged distrusting
immigrants to become naturalized citizens and take
part in the political process in the United States.

Meanwhile, after World War I, Italy had begun
to experiment with political democracy. Tensions
were high and there were many problems when a
former socialist, Benito Mussolini, founded the
Fascist party, the first in Europe. Through violence,
the party grew stronger, and in 1922 Mussolini
became prime minister. A few years later all Italy
was ruled by a system of government Mussolini
called a corporate state. Big business, the Church,

and the state worked together. Workers were denied the right to strike, the secret police crushed political opposition, and children enrolled in semimilitary groups that taught fanatical loyalty to Il Duce ("the Leader"), Benito Mussolini, dictator of Italy.

Well-off Italians who had not considered emigration before now had a reason for leaving. The journalist Max Ascoli was a political refugee who arrived in the United States on a scholarship from the Rockefeller Foundation. He recalled:

> I know exactly the date and the hour when I first realized that all this was bound to happen. It was the night of April 30, 1928, in the police headquarters of a small town in central Italy. I had been brought there, not in a regular state of arrest, but to be questioned—or, as it is said, under protective custody. . . . I had not been locked in a cell, but was invited to spend the night in the office of a clerk, with the door open and two policemen watching from the corridor. I sat at the desk, smoking and looking out of the window until after dawn. I had been caught. They could not pin anything specific on me, yet their hand was on my neck. . . . That pressure had been going on for years, but privately, coming through the channels of friendship or comradeship. From that night on it was going to be exerted by policemen. . . .
>
> At the bottom, I thought, it was a quite simple matter. I had been so far an Italian citizen devoted to his country. Now the police

in their rough way were serving notice on me that my citizenship was going to be forfeited unless I strengthened it by taking a second one. To be an Italian was not enough: one had to become a Fascist. An Italian insisting that the old citizenship was good enough for him was a man without security and rights. I could not become a Fascist. I could not swear allegiance to the Duce. I knew that night that in due course of time fascism was going to make an alien of me. I did not know that in a few years I should have sworn allegiance to the American Constitution and called Italy my former country. But I knew definitely, when the sky over the piazza, out the window of the police headquarters, was all brightened by the fresh clarity of the Italian dawn, that my moorings had been cut and I was on the move.[9]

The Italian physicist Enrico Fermi and his wife, Laura, brought their family to the United States in 1939. Although they were much better off than the millions of immigrants who had preceded them, the Americanization process was not an easy one:

For six months we lived in New York City, within the ten blocks between 110 and 120 streets, where most Columbia University teachers live. Only occasionally did I take a trip downtown, an expedition comparable to that of the villager going to the big city. . . .

Shopping was a cooperative enterprise shared by the maid and me. She could judge the quality of fruit and vegetables, recognize the cuts of meats. I could better translate dollars into lire to decide whether prices were reasonable: I could explore packages and cans, of which I bought large quantities, for, like any newly arrived European, we went on a canned-food spree, which was to last only as long as there were new cans to try.

I patronized the small shops where the clerks could take the time to instruct ignorant foreigners in the marvels of pudding powders and of frozen foods, which had just appeared on the market. In almost every grocery store at least one man was Italian-born or of Italian descent, and with him my maid and I made friends at once. Not that it helped much. Italians in New York come from the south of Italy and they bring to their speech so much of their Neapolitan or Sicilian dialects that it is hard to understand them, whether they speak Italian or English. . . .

In learning the American language and habits, Enrico had a considerable advantage over me: he spent his days at Columbia University among Americans, and inside the physics building he found an obliging mentor in Herbert Anderson, a graduate student who planned to work for his Ph.D. under Enrico's guidance.

No day went by without Enrico's telling me something that Herbert Anderson had taught him.

"Anderson says we should hire our neighbors' children and pay them a penny for each
of our English mistakes they correct. He says
it is the only way of learning the language
efficiently." . . .

In the process of Americanization, however,
there is more than learning language and customs and setting oneself to do whatever Americans can do. There is the absorbing of the
background—the ability to evoke visions of
covered wagons, to hear the sound of thumping
hoofs and jolting wheels over a mountain pass
—the power to relive a miner's excitement in
his boom town in Colorado and to understand
his thoughts when, fifty years later, no longer
a miner but a philosopher, he lets his gaze
float along with the smoke from his pipe over
the ghostlike remnants of his town. The acceptance of New England pride and the participa-
tion in the long-suffering of the South.[10]

Laura Fermi became "Americanized," as did
most of the five million Italian immigrants who have
come to the United States. After the struggle to find
decent jobs, after the bitter encounters with exploitation and prejudice, Italian immigrants stayed and
contributed a great deal to American culture. In
spite of the struggles to become accepted, a surprising number of those who came from Italy recall
their decision to leave with pride and without
regrets.

Constantine Panunzio returned to Italy for a visit

with relatives and it was there that he realized he
had truly become an American:

> Aunt Rose pleaded with me to promise that I
> would remain with her, that at least I would
> remain in Italy as long as she lived. She told
> me that the tract of land and the "casino" on
> it, which she had kept for me all these years,
> was still mine and that I could have it for the
> mere staying and the mere taking. She said that
> she would be so happy if I would only stay
> with her until she died, "only a few years
> more." I remained silent, though not unmoved,
> comforting her with a word now and then. "I
> will come again, aunt," I said. "I will come
> again." She understood! I was no more of this
> fair clime—no more![11]

Later, in Italy during World War I, Panunzio was
moved by the sight of the two flags—Italian and
American—flying side by side:

> Before my eyes the two national standards . . .
> were waving triumphantly in the stiff breeze
> sweeping over the mountain crest. One stood
> for Italy, both ancient and modern, which the
> world respects; for the Italy of my childhood,
> for all the memories of my youth, of loved
> ones, for all that had been beautiful and lovely
> in my boyhood; for the tender memories of
> loved ones, living and dead. The other stood
> for all the suffering of the years, for the awak-
> ening of manhood, for the birth of freedom,

for the unfolding of life. I loved not one the
less, but the other more![12]

Although he was writing about his own experience, Constantine Panunzio managed to capture
what was best about the immigrant experience in
America. Becoming American did not mean denying
one's Italian heritage, but rather adapting it to life
in America. As we have seen, millions of Italian
laborers helped to build America. Others, better
known, became successful businessmen and politicians, entertainers and athletes.

And it is almost impossible to imagine an American who does not sit down, at least occasionally, to
a meal that includes Italian bread or pasta or pizza
or Parmesan cheese or salami—perhaps a glass of
Chianti wine—a legacy from the men and women
who years ago decided to begin new lives in
America.

FROM GREECE

Chapter 5

The Decision to Leave

The southeast corner of Europe—the southernmost part of the Balkan Peninsula that juts into the Mediterranean Sea, and hundreds of neighboring islands—is the cornerstone of Western civilization. The history of Greece, or Hellas, dating from thirty-five hundred years ago, has been turbulent. Greece fought off the Persians in the fifth century B.C. The following century Alexander the Great carried Greek arms and culture all the way to India. But then followed conquest: by the Romans, Byzantines, Franks, and Turks. For two thousand years, until 1829, Greece suffered under one foreign rule or another. But when Greece again became sovereign and independent, the government was anything but stable, and millions of Greeks continued to live under the Turkish rule in lands that were originally Greek.

Throughout this turmoil, however, the cultural creativity of the Greeks was their crowning glory.

Writers, sculptors, painters, and architects flourished during Greece's Golden Age, from 460 to 429 B.C., on a scale never equaled by any country in the world. Greek contributions to law, science, and philosophy laid the foundation for European civilization. With good reason, Greeks have always been intensely proud of their cultural heritage—determined to preserve it and reluctant to leave their native land.

The first Greek known to arrive in America came to Florida with the Spaniards in 1528; his name was Theodoros. No doubt other Greeks made their way to America in the early days of colonization, but there are few records other than the accounts of the New Smyrna colony. Under the auspices of the British Crown, Dr. Andrew Turnbull sailed in 1767 to America with fourteen hundred immigrants—mostly Minorcans and Italians, and some five hundred Greeks—to set up a colony on his great landholdings in Florida. The settlement was named New Smyrna after the birthplace of Turnbull's wife. Many of the immigrants died during the voyage, others succumbed from the extreme hardships of their new life in the colony, and the remainder eventually moved to St. Augustine, the earliest Spanish colony in Florida. One of these immigrants, John Giannopoulos, taught school in St. Augustine, and his restored house, the oldest school in America, still stands there.

Not many Greeks emigrated to the United States before 1900; at that time only 8,515 Greeks were listed by the census. Some who had arrived were unhappy because they were unable to support themselves. Others found the life in America an improvement over the hard village existence they knew in Greece. A young man who emigrated in the late nineteenth century told a magazine interviewer:

> I was born about forty years ago in a little hamlet among the mountains of Laconia in Greece. There were only about 200 people in this place, and they lived in stone huts or cottages, some of which were two stories high, but most of them only one story. The people were shepherds or small farmers, with the exception of the priest and schoolmaster.
>
> Two of the houses pretended to the character of village stores, but they kept only the simplest, cheapest things, and as a general rule, when we wanted to buy anything we had to go down to Sparta, the chief town of our State, which was two hours' walk away from our village. There was not even a blacksmith shop in our town.
>
> But the people did very well without shops. They made almost everything for themselves. The inside of the cottage consisted of one large room with a board floor. Sometimes there were partitions inside the cottage, making several rooms, but everything was very simple. The fireplace at one end of the room was large and open; beds were made of boards covered with

hay, and stools and tables comprised about all the remainder of the furniture. Cooking was done on an iron tripod with the fire underneath.

Cotton goods we bought in Sparta, but we seldom bought anything else. We made all our own clothing, shearing the sheep, washing the wool, carding, spinning and weaving by hand as they did in the time of Homer. We made our own wheat and oats into flour and meal and did our own baking.

Our farms varied in size from ten to forty acres, and we raised on them such things as are raised here in America—all the grains and most of the fruits and vegetables. We plowed with oxen, thrashed with flails, winnowed by hand, and ground our grain in a mortar.

We had very little money, and so little use for money that the currency might almost as well have been the iron sort of our remote forefathers.

There was a little school in the town—there are schools all over Greece now—and most of the people could read and write, so they were not entirely ignorant; yet they had small knowledge of the world, and there were many, especially among the women, who knew almost nothing of what lay beyond the boundaries of their farms.[1]

Further Greek immigration was negligible until the 1880s when hundreds came each year. In 1891 more than a thousand Greeks entered the United

The Ellis Island Immigrant Station was opened in 1892. In the next fifty years some sixteen million immigrants passed through it. (A meal at Ellis Island. Courtesy of the Williams Collection, New York Public Library.)

The first American institution most immigrant families met was the public school system. (Saluting the flag in the Mott Street Industrial School, c. 1889–90. Photo by Jacob Riis. Courtesy of the Museum of the City of New York.)

Southern Italians valued the family above all else. (Italian family at dinner, 1915. Photo by Lewis Hine. Courtesy of the New York Public Library.)

The pick and shovel became the symbol of Italian workers. They helped to build the nation's railroads, dig the subways, pave the roads. (Group of Italian street laborers working under the Sixth Avenue elevated, New York City, 1910. Photo by Lewis Hine. Courtesy of the New York Public Library.)

Jacob Riis worked as a journalist-photographer in New York around the turn of the century. Little Italy appeared to an outsider as a sprawling slum. (Baxter Street Court, 22 Baxter Street. Photo by Jacob Riis. Courtesy of the Museum of the City of New York.)

About ninety-five percent of the Greeks who emigrated from 1899 to 1910 were males. (Greek restaurant, Bowery, 1904. Photo by Byron. Courtesy of the Museum of the City of New York.)

In Chicago, Hull House was a settlement house known for its charitable, cultural, and social works. It was especially important to the new immigrants. (The Greek wrestling club at Hull House, 1910. Photo by Lewis Hine. Courtesy of the New York Public Library.)

Old traditions carry on in the Greek Orthodox Church today. (A young man re-trieves the cross in the Sanctification of Waters Ceremony, New York Harbor, Feast of the Epiphany, 1980. Courtesy of the *Daily News*.)

As soon as there was any significant number of Greeks living in a particular area, one of them opened a coffeehouse. (Greek coffeehouse today in Astoria, Queens. Photo by Diane Tong.)

Magnificent ritual. (Greek Orthodox Archdiocesan Cathedral of the Holy Trinity, New York City. Photo by Costa Hayden. Courtesy of the Greek Orthodox Archdiocese of North and South America.)

Greeks tended to save their money and set up in small business. (A typical neighborhood establishment in Manhattan, Joe Jr.'s Greek Restaurant, Sixth Avenue and 12th Street. Photo by an anonymous customer.)

Today the "Ironbound" section of Newark, New Jersey, is an ethnic Portuguese center. (In 1915 Portuguese and other immigrants played sandlot baseball in an early type of playground. Photo by Lewis Hine. Courtesy of the New York Public Library.)

People of Portuguese descent have enriched American life. (An advertisement for the West Brighton Beach Hotel, c. 1890, showing John Philip Sousa conducting his band. Courtesy of the Museum of the City of New York.)

Portuguese Day in Newark, New Jersey. (Photo courtesy of Luso-Americano.)

The Civil War (1936–39) brought agony to Spain. The Spanish artist Pablo Picasso immortalized the bombing of the town of Guernica in his painting. (*Guernica* [1937, May–early June]. Oil on canvas. On extended loan to The Museum of Modern Art, New York, from the estate of the artist.)

Confirmation at Our Lady of Fatima, Newark, New Jersey. (Photo courtesy of Luso-Americano.)

For hundreds of years Basques have been herding sheep in the Pyrenees. They have continued this vocation in the Rocky Mountains. (Getting ready for shipping. Highland Sheep Company, Emmett, Idaho. Photo by I. Eigurea.)

The Basques keep up their traditional ways in America. Here they pursue a special pleasure—dancing. (Oinkari Basque Dancers. Boise, Idaho. Photo by Paul Acorda.)

States. These new arrivals were almost exclusively men looking for temporary employment, men who intended to return to Greece and their families after making their fortunes. However, many of them stayed, creating predominantly male communities. In Chicago the newly founded Hull House, a settlement house known for its charitable, cultural, and social works, was located in the middle of the Greek quarter and was especially important to the new immigrants.

During the next thirty years nearly a half million Greeks emigrated to the United States. Most of the people in Greece earned their living farming, even though on three quarters of the land farming was impossible because of mountains or lack of irrigation. During the 1890s the demand for currants—Greece's principal export—dropped dramatically. The French and Russian crops had recovered from the devastation of phylloxera. Farmers who had destroyed olive trees in order to plant the more profitable crop of currants were faced with years of waiting for new trees to bear marketable fruit.

Greece was a poor country. The government squandered public money and taxed the peasantry beyond endurance. One immigrant in Philadelphia complained of "taxes on taxes without seeing any improvement."[2] Peasants who tried to borrow money to buy land found interest rates of seventy to eighty percent. Fathers and brothers were obliged to provide their daughters and sisters with an appropriate dowry. A dowry meant material goods and property and indicated the value of the bride. This

system of exchange between families was funda-
mental to the economic and social functioning of
many societies. It still exists today in many countries. Hundreds of thousands of Greeks left,
especially for the United States. For many, America
seemed to provide a chance to save enough money.

Families in Greece began to hear positive stories
about America from relatives and neighbors who
had emigrated to find work. One immigrant wrote
his former employer in Greece:

> Here the people work much and regularly, and
> rest only on Sunday, but we fare well. This
> day that I am writing you is Sunday; I took
> my bath, had my milk, and I will pass the day
> satisfactorily. Where did I know life with such
> order? . . . If you wish, afentiko [master], you
> can do well to come, and I will send you the
> cost of the ticket.[3]

Moneylenders, employers' agents, steamship lines,
and even the Greek government described the
United States as a place with unlimited opportunities. Young people were urged to enrich themselves
by emigrating:

> Why remain here to struggle for a piece of
> bread without any security for the future,
> without honor and independence? Why not
> open your eyes and see the good that awaits
> you; harden your heart and seek your fortune
> abroad, where so many of your countrymen
> already have made theirs?

Why linger? To protect your parents? Today or tomorrow, whether their children are here or abroad, they will close their eyes forever. It will be better for you to leave home and send a little money to provide for them in their advancing years.

Or are you waiting to cultivate the barren lands with the ploughshare and dig in the fields? Have you seen how much progress you have made thus far?[4]

Many answered the call during the peak years for Greek immigration from 1901 to 1920. At the end of the Balkan Wars in 1913, when Greece had joined with its neighboring countries to rid themselves of Turkish domination, Greece reacquired its lost lands. The overburdened economy was hard pressed by these new populations and in addition had to cope with hordes of refugees from the Turks. An amazing exchange of population brought a million and a quarter Greeks in Anatolia back home in return for four hundred thousand Turks who had resided in Greek territories.

In 1921 the quota system for European countries was established, and the Immigration Act of 1924 limited Greek immigration to 308 per year.

However, after World War II the restrictions were lifted. During the war Greece drove out Mussolini's Italian invaders and continued to fight a guerilla war during the later German occupation. The guerillas, made up mainly of left-wing groups and Communists, eventually controlled most of the country.

The country was ravaged: hundreds of villages were burned and hundreds of thousands of people were homeless and in need of aid.

In 1944 the British occupied most of Greece. Working with right-wing forces in an attempt to keep communism from spreading further in the Balkans, they helped to drive the guerillas to the north of Athens. King George II returned from exile in 1946 and formed a government, and upon his death the next year, his brother Paul became king.

The guerillas in the north persisted in their activities against the government, and in 1947 civil war broke out. Taking over from the British, the United States poured in hundreds of millions of dollars of aid to the Greek government, and in 1949, the rebel guerillas backed by the Communist regimes in Yugoslavia, Albania, and Bulgaria gave up the fight. Both sides had sustained enormous casualties, and the already weakened Greek economy was further devastated by the civil conflict. The United States permitted some of the displaced persons and refugees to enter. Between 1946 and 1960 more than fifty-six thousand came.

They were much different from the peasant farmers who had arrived earlier. Many were skilled workers, shipowners, merchants, teachers, and students. Achilles Manolakis, who originally came in 1957 as a high school exchange student, returned in 1963 as a graduate student. In many ways it was easier for him to adjust to his new surroundings than for his countrymen who had come in earlier years:

> The main reason I left Greece was to continue my graduate education. And while I was doing that, then I decided that I would like to stay here. There were many reasons—one of them was better research opportunities. . . .
>
> And then slowly, for reasons I don't know, I started thinking of staying here permanently and less and less of going back to Greece. . . . I applied to become a resident. A few years later I applied to become a citizen.[5]

Between 1967 and 1974, Greece was ruled by a ruthless military dictatorship, the fascist government of "the colonels." They imposed strict censorship, a ban on labor strikes and public meetings, and tortured and killed all who spoke against them. For the first time since 1920 more than ten thousand Greeks entered the United States each year. During that seven-year period more than a hundred thousand arrived.

In August 1967 George Kokkas, a tool and die maker, came to the United States for a visit. Deciding that he liked this country, he returned with his wife and children on a permanent visa in 1969. He seemed to believe that neither the exiled king nor the new military rulers had his interests in mind:

> In Greece I had my own machine shop. But the situation with the war in 1967 was very bad. The political system in Greece—the king and the prime ministers fought each other, so they didn't take care of the people, only of themselves.

Work over there was very bad. In those days, a worker in Greece made about five dollars a day, when a worker's pay in the United States was about thirty dollars a day. But the reason I came to the United States was because the situation in Greece was bad. And I was concerned about the education of my kids. Greece in those days had only one university, and if you had kids who wanted to go to the university it was very hard to get the chance.[6]

Altogether more than six hundred thousand Greeks have emigrated to the United States. They came for a variety of reasons, but since the Greeks have one of the lowest levels of per capita income in Europe, economics was the main reason. Many returned to Greece—some two hundred thousand—when the colonels were overthrown in 1974, and democracy was restored to the country that had given the world the word: *demos* meaning common people and *kratia* from *kratos,* meaning strength and power.

Chapter 6

Making a Living

Although there were some skilled workers and some professionals among the more than 350,000 Greeks who came to America between 1891 and 1920, the majority had been poor peasant farmers in Greece. After making the decision to leave, the next step was raising money for the voyage to America.

Relatives already living in the United States frequently sent money "home" to pay for the trip. Other emigrants borrowed from moneylenders—often men who had returned from America with money they had managed to save—or against their family farms. Some sold their farms to raise money, but since most emigrants planned to stay in America only a few years, the most popular way of raising money was borrowing—at high interest rates.

Once the arrangements were made, the trip itself was arduous. The two main ports in Greece were Piraeus, just outside Athens, and Patras. From one of those towns, voyagers had to journey to Naples, or some other European port, and change ships for the trip to America. Not until 1907 was a direct steamship line established from Piraeus.

Most Greek peasants traveled in steerage and endured dirty, overcrowded conditions. Sam Fortosis said his 1914 trip

> was awful. The boats were then—they used to call them cattle boats. It took thirty days to cross the Atlantic. Plus a couple of days from Greece to Italy. . . . Because of the rough sea, the boat couldn't go ahead. In fact, it was four or five days that we were going backward instead of forward. All the Greeks that were there—maybe forty, fifty, or sixty—were all single. They were either married and left their wives over there, or were seamen like me.[1]

A writer aboard one ship noted:

> Many of them left their village for the first time and for the first time had seen the ocean which terrified them even when it was calm. They were melancholy and sat in small groups and spoke slowly. Every one of them must have been thinking of the village he left behind, his wife, his children, his parents.[2]

In spite of the rural background of most of the Greek immigrants, the majority concentrated in urban areas. As early as 1900 at least half the Greeks living in the United States had settled in Chicago, Boston, Philadelphia, San Francisco,

Savannah, and Lowell, Massachusetts. As more
Greeks arrived, they too headed for the cities. By
1920 Chicago, New York, Detroit, San Francisco,
and Lowell had the largest Greek populations in the
country.

After passing inspection at Ellis Island, Greeks
with relatives or neighbors in America set out to
join them. Greeks who did not have friends or
relatives in this country needed to find a job that did
not require mastery of the English language. Some
worked on railroad gangs or in factories or inde-
pendently as bootblacks, pushcart peddlers, or con-
fectioners. Most did not remain laborers for long.
Unlike most immigrants, Greeks tended to save
their money and set themselves up in small businesses, such as fruit stores. Many struck it rich.

Naturally, everyone did not strike it rich. Some
were the victims of a padrone system similar to the
one that plagued Italian immigrants. With Greek
immigrants the padrone system often extended to
the shoe-shining trade, and the fruit, flower, or
vegetable peddlers in the larger cities. For instance,
the Greek owner of a shoeshine parlor would return
to his hometown for a visit and arrange for boys to
emigrate to America and work for him. The padrone
would lend the boy sufficient money to get to
America and then, much like an indentured servant,
the boy was obliged to work a certain number of
years for the padrone. Many of the boys were exploited. A probation officer in Cincinnati described
such a situation in 1911:

A Greek boy complained to the Humane Society that his employer made him work from half-past six in the morning until eleven at night, took away his tips, half starved him, and refused to pay even his meager wages of thirty-five cents per day until the end of the year in order to prevent his leaving. An investigation was made, and fifteen other boys were found to be living in exactly the same conditions as the complainant. . . .

The other case was that of August Nicolas, aged seventeen, who was brought before the Juvenile Court of Cincinnati, August 29, 1911, charged with stealing fifty dollars from his father, George Nicolas. Upon interrogation, August stated that his real father was dead, that George Nicolas was his stepfather, and that he came to this country in March, 1909, to work for him as a bootblack, at twelve dollars a month and board. He said he had not received a penny, nothing but a few cheap clothes and board, and that consequently he considered himself entitled to the money he had taken.

He also stated that he and the four boys employed with him occupied one room and one bed, that the others received twelve dollars, but that they were compelled to turn over their tips to George Nicolas. Their hours, he said, were from sixteen to seventeen per day, Sundays included. Asked why he had not sought employment elsewhere, he replied that

Nicolas, Sr., had warned them that according to the laws of this country they would be arrested if they left his employ.[3]

Laws against contract labor and influential Greek-language newspapers that waged a tough campaign against padrones gradually helped to curb the system. But as late as 1916, Christos Damascus, the editor of *Saloniki* in Chicago, was still crusading against the padrones:

> There are certain rich bosses who fill their teeth with gold, that they may eat more easily with the profits earned . . . by the sweat and blood of young Greek boys. The Greeks were ready to fight the Turks and Bulgars for enslaving and degrading their countrymen, still they had no scruples about enslaving their own youth in the shoeshining parlors of the United States.[4]

Not only boys were exploited by the padrone system. Some men posed as padrones and took money from Greeks for jobs that did not exist. One recruited for his brother in Kansas City:

> "Go to my brother who will give you work at a dollar sixty-five a day on the railroad he manages," was his advice to three innocent prospects. "But we don't have the money to pay for our passage," replied the three. "I will provide you with tickets," answered the agent, "which cost five hundred and fifty drachmas [$110] each, if each of you turn your lands

over to me as security, and I will send you [to the United States] with a warranty, so that you will not be rejected by the authorities, because I have arranged with the transoceanic ship that will take you to New Orleans and not to New York; I shall also guarantee you work with my brother at a dollar sixty-five a day, and I am sure that in two or three months you will be able to pay your debt. You can pay the money to my brother in Kansas, it is the same."[5]

The three agreed and emigrated to America. They did reach Kansas City, but were laid off after just thirteen days of work. They complained to authorities, with no success; in fact, they learned they had been overcharged by 295 drachmas [$59] for the trip.

As with the Italians, there were attempts made to convince Greek immigrants to bypass the padrone system and become farmers, particularly in California. Many did decide to live in the San Francisco Bay area—there were 5,000 by 1908—but very few went into farming. Anastasios Mountanos, the editor of a Greek-language newspaper in San Francisco, who tried to convince the immigrants to change their ways, was able by 1919 to single out about 650 Greeks who were working as farmers in California. Most Greeks wanted no part of it; they associated it with the poverty in Greece. The place of opportunity was the city.

About ninety-five percent of the Greeks who

emigrated from 1899 to 1910 were males. They set up housekeeping in the tenements of the big cities. A detailed description of their living arrangement appeared in the 1914 *Report of the Massachusetts Commission on Immigration.*

> The men hire an apartment, or sometimes a house, and share the rent, which generally amounts to between $1.50 and $2.50 a month for each. Sometimes one of the men acts as boss, and runs the apartment for the others, cooking the meals himself perhaps. A few instances were found where the boss was married, or where his sister lived with him. In three of the twenty-three Greek groups visited, a woman was living. . . . In most of the groups visited . . . the men do their own cooking, either acting each one as his own commissary, or taking turns at buying and cooking the food. Occasionally, . . . the men eat at restaurants or coffee-houses.
>
> As is to be expected under the circumstances, the living and sleeping conditions of these men are far from good. In most cases economy leads them to choose houses for which rents are low, and which consequently are often in a most dilapidated condition. These houses are planned for a family of four or five persons, and are totally unsuited for the purposes to which they are put. The sanitary conditions are far from adequate; the furnishings are often the poorest possible.

Moreover, as the rooms receive the minimum of care and attention from the men, the apartments are seldom clean and are sometimes filthy. The sleeping quarters are, of course, crowded. Frequently the floor is covered with mattresses and pillows, and clothes are scattered about the rooms.[6]

Living conditions for those who worked at railroad construction were no better. The employer provided housing in boxcars at the site of the job, for a price.

The men lived this way for a while, and then either sent for their wives or began looking for one. Greece was becoming a country with a surplus of women, and many began to emigrate, hoping to find husbands among the Greeks in the United States. One woman in 1908 explained:

I came to America in 1908 because my father was unable to provide me with a dowry. There were few Greek women in the country then and the men went begging for wives of their own nationality and religion.[7]

Gradually, the enclaves of men gave way to family units. A surprising number of the men moved from jobs as day laborers into successful independent businesses. Even though George Vordakis, a ship's engineer, arrived in 1958, his story is typical. He landed in New York with two hundred dollars in his pocket and began work as a delivery boy. He went to night school to learn English and kept looking for an opportunity to do better:

> So in the meantime, I worked as a car hop in a drive-in restaurant at nights. One day, somebody told me about a place in Hightstown [N.J.] for sale. We came down and saw the place and I asked the man how much he wanted. He said so much. I said, "Fine. I'll let you know in a few days." The next day we went back. We said we're going to buy the place. We called our lawyer and I explained that the man wanted $40,000 for the place, and that he wanted $10,000 down.
>
> My lawyer said, "You're crazy. You don't have one penny to your name, so you're going to go and buy forty thousand dollars worth of business?"
>
> I said, "Don't worry about it. I have faith in me and I have faith in my wife."
>
> My father-in-law said, "Well, I have some money in the basement"—he never believed in the bank. So he handed me the down payment for the business.
>
> Two years later, I decided to build an ice cream place. Now we owed $20,000, some thousand dollars to the guy we took the mortgage from. I went to the bank and I said, "Well, I want to build an ice cream place next to Stewart's."
>
> He said, "Well the property's not worth the

money you want." I asked him for $55,000. He said, "I don't know if we'll be able to give you the $55,000 you're asking."

I said, "Well, if you don't give it to me, I'll have to find the money. I'll have to knock on some doors to find the money because I feel I need the place. I'd like to build the place, and I'm going to go someplace else if you say no."

Two days later, they called me up to pick up the $55,000. Amazing, you know? So when I picked up the check, he said to me, "Normally we don't do that for anybody, but I admire your guts, you know, the way you came and asked for money."

So I said, "Thank you very much." And since then everything rolls toward me.[8]

Chapter 7

Settling In

Although many Greeks did well in the United States, it is also true that nearly forty percent of those who came returned to Greece to live. But they were not the only immigrants to return to their native lands. From 1908 to 1931 more than four million (including over one million Italians) people of all nationalities left, presumably to return home.

Some were angered by the discrimination of the native-born Americans. The most serious attack against a Greek community took place in Omaha, Nebraska, in 1909. *The Greek Star* wrote:

> These most unfortunate happenings began when a Greek in Omaha, by the name of John Masouridis, killed a policeman. Because of this, a huge demonstration was organized by lawyers, congressmen, city officials, and other prominent citizens, in front of the city hall. They discussed the murder under great tension;

then, advised and encouraged, the enraged mob of Omaha proceeded to avenge the blood of the slain policeman by attacking and driving out all Greeks indiscriminately.

Naturally, no intelligent and cool-headed American would approve of such action, nor would he praise the barbarous acts of mob violence which were perpetrated against quiet and law-abiding Greeks. However, no sympathetic voice was raised among the Americans, with but a few exceptions, to defend the mistreated and beaten Greeks. . . .

Whatever we Greeks say or do at this time will be in vain, because what has been done cannot be undone; nor can the voice of the weak prevail over the "rights" of the strong.

Only a few years ago, the Greeks of Chicago were looked down upon whenever some Greek violated the law, especially when some crime was committed. We ask: Were all the Greeks to blame for the acts of one or a few lawbreakers? Much intolerance, prejudice, and contempt have been directed against the Greeks of Chicago on the part of the native, older Americans, or other immigrant groups. By and large, this spirit of hatred and intolerance was not justified.

Not only the Greeks of Chicago, but those in every part of the country have protested the indiscriminate persecution of the Greeks of Omaha; first, because these attacks were unjust and brutal; and second, because this practice might spread further by arousing the American public against all the Greek immigrants in every part of the country.[1]

Anti-Greek sentiment never approached the level of anti-Italian sentiment, but all immigrants were wary of slurs against their ethnic backgrounds. Sam Fortosis recalls:

Of course we had it tough, not only the Greeks but a lot of the minorities. You know, America wasn't like it is today. . . . You couldn't mix. I tell you why you couldn't mix, because in the little towns . . . if you were Greek or Italian you were considered low class, very low class, because you couldn't speak English. And they didn't know anything about the Greeks. We weren't welcome over here. If you weren't strong enough to fight, you just got a lickin' and put your tail under your two legs and went. In other words, we took it. We couldn't give it back. But when we could speak a few words of English and got a little stronger, we started giving it back.

Then I went into the service. I went to the First World War. On the troop train, there was a boy—I guess he was of Swedish descent—and he said to me: "You know what they call you?" I said, "No." He said, "A wop." I didn't know what "wop" meant. It really doesn't mean anything, but it doesn't mean anything good either. So I said: "Is that good or bad?" He said, "Not too good." Well, I

called him a name—I don't want to repeat it.
And I said, "Don't you ever say that again
because it's no good." He didn't say that again.
And we went to Georgia; we went to Boston;
and we came back to Long Beach, Long
Island—but he never said that again. In other
words, he respected me.[2]

Sam Fortosis stayed in America, and most of the
Greeks who left did not give discrimination as the
reason. One man said: "One reason I came back
was to get married. It was difficult to marry a Greek
woman in the United States in those days."[3] And
another: "Those who married women of another
nationality found it difficult to get along with them.
The religious question made it difficult for me to
marry one of a different nationality. Greek women
are soft. They are not as bold as American women.
They respect Greek customs and traditions. Religion
and nationality are deeply ingrained in them from
youth."[4]

Still others complained of the hard work in
America: "I worked too hard. I was a fruit peddler
and climbed many stairs. The United States was
good to me. But I got tired of rising early in the
morning to go to the green market and climbing the
stairs I climbed in Chicago."[5]

Many returned to Greece for a visit and ended up
staying there. "I just came for a short visit in
1932. . . . But a friend of mine persuaded me to
stay. In 1935 I was married. I should never have

returned to Greece."[6] Another repatriated Greek was happier about his choice. "My father died and I had an orphan sister. I had some property I was interested in. I planned to stay six months because I had a six-months leave of absence from my job. I helped my sister get married and I was married too. Life appealed to me in Greece."[7]

Even immigrants who had been successful in the United States looked back on the quality of their lives in Greece with fondness. Anastasia Stephanios recalled:

> Greek people like all the time to have good times and drink and dance and not work as hard as American people. No. In Greece, at two o'clock everybody comes home to eat and sleep until four o'clock in the afternoon. At four o'clock they get up to go back to work, and they come home seven o'clock. At ten o'clock they come home to eat and have a good time. They don't work hard, not the way American people do. I think that's much better, more quiet. American people get too excited because they work hard. I see my husband—he works sixteen hours a day. I don't go any place; I don't have any good times, nothing. I stay home because I don't have anybody to bring me. After my husband is off, we go some places. I've got a house, a big house, and I'm all alone. I don't have any servants because it's too expensive. I stay home

and cook, wash, scrub the floors, and I can't take my children to the movies. No. It's different—you know, I came from a village— I'm different.[8]

Anastasia Stephanios, and thousands of other Greeks, remained in the United States and kept their customs and traditions to a greater extent than most immigrants. As soon as there was any significant number of Greeks living in a particular area, one of them opened a coffeehouse. J. P. Xenides described them this way:

> Coffee-houses provide the principal recreation for me. People flock to these places day and night, sitting around tables, sipping black coffee, smoking cigars, or more commonly cigarettes . . . and discussing everything— business, news of national interest, and of course the politics of Greece and the attitude of Americans towards them. At times they discuss American politics. There are often animated discussions that might be taken for quarrels by those who do not understand Greek, but it is all verbal, no blows exchanged excepting the blows the tables or chairs receive.[9]

A reporter for the *San Francisco Examiner* in 1923 noted:

> If you want to find the social center of the San Francisco Greek colony, you will immedi-

ately set out for the coffee house in the vicinity
of Third and Folsom Streets. There is a Greek
population here of approximately 11,500 and
there are 26 coffee houses.[10]

Coffeehouses were at their peak when Greek men
were here and very few women. Some in the most
populated areas furnished music for their patrons.
Others showed movies, or held floor shows or strong
man exhibitions. A few turned into gambling houses
and were periodically raided by the police. But on
the whole, coffeehouses provided comfortable
refuges for men who worked hard all day and slept
in dingy, crowded quarters at night.

One sure subject of discussion among coffeehouse patrons was the local Greek-language newspaper. In Greece there was a saying, "Either you
give me a job or I'll bring out a newspaper."[11]
Historians have determined that Greeks produced
more newspapers in proportion to their numbers
than any other ethnic group. There were five in the
San Francisco area, for instance.

But the first, and most famous, Greek newspaper
was *Atlantis,* founded in 1894 by Solon Vlasto.
Vlasto had emigrated to New York in 1873 at the
age of twenty-one. His first job was at a confec-
tionary factory, but within a year he had taken a job
with a profitable steamship line. The *Atlantis* was
successful from the start. Its chief rival—and there
were many—was the *National Herald,* founded in
1915. The two papers held opposing views of the

political situation in Greece, and their editorials provided the fuel for heated debates at the coffee-houses.

The newspapers kept the Greek language alive, which was important to most Greek immigrants. They worried about their children learning English in public schools and forgetting the Greek language. They wanted to give their "American-born children . . . the greatness of our race . . . teach them the Greek language and impose upon them Greek character and Greek virtue."[12] Consequently, many Greek children came home from public school and went directly to Greek school. One such institution was the Korais School in Chicago:

> The Korais school is one of the many schools all over the country. The object of the school is not to mold perfect Greeks, but perfect Greek-Americans. The English and Greek languages are taught side by side; Greek and American ideas are taught, reading, writing, English, history, geography, composition, religion, etc. . . .
>
> The pupils, besides their educational lessons, are taught music and dancing. . . . the result is not only perpetuating Greek religion, language, and nationalism, but also Americanizing the pupils by the best possible method.[13]

Most Greek schools were funded and operated by the Greek Orthodox Church. As soon as a community could afford it, it sent for a priest from Greece, where, until the 1950s, all were born, reared, and educated. The Church became a constant reminder of home, and the ceremonies, unique in the United States, gave them a greater sense of community.

The Greek Orthodox Church, which is part of the Eastern Orthodox Church, followed in the footsteps of the Russian Orthodox Church in America. Originally allied with the Roman Catholic Church, the Eastern Church rebelled against the idea of the primacy of the pope and broke away in the eleventh century. The Greek Orthodox Church follows the Julian calendar, and its parish priests may marry. Old traditions of ritual and art carry on in the Church today, which next to the Roman Catholic Church, has more members than any other single church in America.

Ariadne Thompson recalled her grandfather, a Greek Orthodox priest born in Ithaca in 1840:

> On Sundays Grandfather officiated at the Greek Orthodox Church. On these occasions he attained a kind of magnificence in our eyes, for he was always attired in long, colored robes made of stiff silk embroidered with gold thread. Around his neck there hung a heavy, jeweled cross, and in his hand he held an incense burner, ornately worked in gold, which he swung by three bronze chains. On his head he wore a high, satin hat, curved in front and embroidered with gold.
>
> The whole church smelled of incense and candle wax and flowers. From time to time the

choir would sing in a queer, minor, quavering chant, echoing the words of Byzantine music—a high, nasal, grievous intonation that sustained a note of anguish. In the midst of lighted candles, against a backdrop of a huge crucifix inscribed with the letters INRI, Grandfather would raise his hand in benediction over the bowed heads of the congregation and murmur, in a kind of mystic monotone, the words of the Lord's Prayer in Greek. . . .

Two or three times a year Grandfather would bless the house. On these occasions the family would gather together and follow him from room to room, standing with bowed heads and making the sign of the cross as he swung the incense burner from side to side, supplicating the Lord, in His divine mercy, to bring peace, love and prosperity to this house. Always afterward, for a whole day, a kind of benevolence seemed to fall over the household, and there would not be a cross word spoken.[14]

The Church remained important to immigrants who came to America much later. Achilles Manolakis said:

There are times when people from Greece or of Greek background create . . . a very strong feeling of togetherness, for example, on certain religious holidays. . . .

In spite of making a choice of living away from Greece, I personally cannot ignore those events or those customs, or whatever it may be.

And then having some Greeks around is a very important thing.

One thing that comes to my mind is celebrating Greek Easter. Greek Easter is the most important and the holiest holy day for Greek Orthodox. It is more important in a way than Christmas. In the rest of the Christian world, Christmas is considered most important. I don't know how it developed to be the most important thing . . . Christmas comes in the winter, and Easter comes in the Spring. And the Spring is more pleasant than winter. In any case, Easter in Greece is celebrated in the Spring by everybody going to church. There is a midnight service and everybody goes there. In fact, there is not enough room in the church for that, so everybody goes in the streets, where you hear the service from the loudspeakers. And after midnight, they go home and they have Easter soup, which is some concoction that you eat once a year. I don't think that you would like to eat it more than once a year. That day it tastes great. And you have firecrackers and fireworks and everybody is kissing each other and celebrating and singing. And you have Easter eggs which you hold in your hand and somebody else comes with another and hits it from the top and sees whose egg will break first.

Children get new clothes. Easter time is a time when . . . you switch from your winter clothes to your summer clothes. It's a very

open type of holiday. It's associated in a way
with a rebirth, rebirth of everything, not only
the religious aspects of the resurrection of
Christ, but the rebirth of the nation in a way,
the rebirth of each individual. It's essentially
a combination of both religious and pagan
points of view. By pagan I mean the celebration of spring. Easter is very special.[15]

In addition to the Church many secular clubs—
both local and national—were formed to help
Greeks in America. The largest and most influential
were the Panhellenic Union, founded in 1907;
AHEPA (American Hellenic Educational Progressive Association), founded in 1922; and GAPA
(Greek American Progressive Association), founded
in 1923.

The Greeks who stayed, then, retained close ties
to Greece and a strong sense of identity as Greeks.
They blended this with their experiences in America,
creating a special sense of what it means to be a
Greek-American, comfortable in America and in
Greece too.

George Kokkas is an American now by choice,
but his native land is still part of him, the heritage
that he brought with him:

A lot of people still call me Greek, old George
the Greek. And I say, "No, I'm an American
citizen. I'm no Greek." Really I'm Greek because I was born in Greece, and I felt that
yesterday I was Greek. Only with the [citizen-
ship papers] am I American. I came to this

country when I was forty years old, and I can't
forget very easily the country where I spent my
first forty years.[16]

George Kokkas, and thousands of other Greek
immigrants, have enriched life in America by honor-
ing the ideals of their native land in their new
homeland.

FROM PORTUGAL

Chapter 8

A Long Tradition

Although the total number of Portuguese immigrants in the United States did not approach that of the Italians, or even the Greeks, by the 1970s over 360,000 Portuguese had settled in America. Modern-day Portuguese were only following in the tradition of their ancestors, who had started sailing as early as the sixth century to the Azores and Madeira, islands that were eventually colonized in the fifteenth century. Portuguese sailors accompanied Columbus—who had studied map making in Lisbon—on his voyage of discovery, and the Portuguese led all nations in the exploring of and fishing in the Newfoundland area and the Grand Banks. In 1500 Pedro Álvares Cabral, sailing to India via the Cape of Good Hope, reached South America and claimed Brazil for Portugal.

A native of Portugal may have been the first European to settle in New England. The Dighton Rock, discovered in 1926 on the banks of the

Taunton River in Berkley, Massachusetts, bears this inscription:

MIGUEL CORTEREAL V DEI
HIC DUX IND 1511[1]

Translated, the inscription says "Miguel Corte-Real, by the will of God here chief of the Indians, 1511." Some historians believe that Miguel Corte-Real, a Portuguese explorer from the Azore Islands, was shipwrecked off the coast of New England in 1502, and that after he and his crew came ashore they settled down to live with the friendly Wampanoag Indians, who made Corte-Real their chief. The marker would have been made by his followers at the time of his death.

Whether or not Corte-Real was a Wampanoag chief, Portuguese explorers and seamen did reach North American shores during the sixteenth century. João Rodriguez Cabrillo explored the California coast and discovered San Diego Bay in 1542.

The first recorded Portuguese settlement in North America was in 1654, when a group of Jewish refugees from Recife, Brazil, arrived in New Amsterdam (later renamed New York). Their ancestors had left Portugal nearly 150 years earlier to escape persecution by the Catholic Church. At first they settled in Holland; then, when the Dutch West India Company conquered the northeastern part of Brazil in the 1630s, many of the Jews emigrated to Brazil. But by 1654 Brazil had been reconquered by Portugal and was no longer safe for Jews. When twenty-three Jews arrived in New

Amsterdam, Peter Stuyvesant, the governor of the colony, wrote to his employers:

> The Jews who have arrived would nearly all like to remain here, but . . . owing to their present indigence they might become a charge in the coming winter, we have . . . deemed it useful to require them in a friendly way to depart.[2]

The Jews petitioned the governor to permit them to stay:

> Your Honors should also please consider that many of the Jewish nation are principal share-holders in the Company. They have always striven their best for the company, and many of their nation have lost immense and great capital in its shares and obligations.[3]

The Dutch company in control of New Amsterdam wrote to Governor Stuyvesant:

> After having further weighed and considered the matter, we observe that this [expelling the Jews] would be somewhat unreasonable and unfair, especially because of the considerable loss sustained by this nation, with others, in the taking of Brazil, as also because of the large amount of capital which they still have invested in the shares of this company.[4]

Those Portuguese Jewish refugees were the founders of the American Jewish community. The oldest Jewish cemeteries in the United States, in New York City and in Newport, Rhode Island, have gravestones with Portuguese inscriptions, and the congregations in those two cities used the Portuguese language until the latter half of the eighteenth century.

Portuguese immigration to the United States began in greater numbers about 1830 with the recruiting of Portuguese seamen by the captains of whaling ships from New England. By the 1850s the New Bedford, Massachusetts, fleet numbered 329 ships and employed ten thousand seamen, many of whom were Portuguese. A number of Azoreans took part in the gold rush in California, and others went there to work in the mines and the lumber mills. They arrived on sailing ships that had gone around Cape Horn.

In 1894 a Provincetown, Massachusetts, newspaper noted:

> The Provincetown fleet is manned exclusively by Portuguese. . . . Captains and crews are all, or nearly all, Azoreans, and from a mere handful in 1840, the Portuguese population has increased to upward of 2,000 in 1894. . . . They take kindly to the sea and make excellent fishermen.[5]

The country of Portugal has a long coastline facing the Atlantic, and the Portuguese had always been redoubtable sailors and fishermen. The novelist Mary Heaton Vorse wrote in 1911:

> In the heyday of the whaling business, when
> the big fleet of whalers went out from
> Provincetown on voyages to the South Seas
> after the whale and the sea elephant, when our
> coasters plied from Boston to the Indies, our
> skippers stopped at the Western Islands to
> recruit their crews, and the Portuguese men
> who were landed in Provincetown from our
> vessels found there was more money to be
> made in this country, and sent for their wives
> and children or their sweethearts.[6]

The whaling captains from New England and the
San Francisco Bay area, having lost men because of
desertion or illness, would stop at Horta, a port on
the island of Fayal in the Azores, and later at the
Cape Verde island of Brava, in order to sign up new
crew members. In time many of the Portuguese seamen themselves became ship captains and owners.
Still, by 1880 the census noted only a little more
than fifteen thousand Portuguese living in America,
split about evenly between California and Massachusetts and Rhode Island.

The second period of Portuguese immigration
runs from 1880 to 1920. When the whaling industry
declined because the discovery of oil meant whale
oil was no longer needed for fuel, the Portuguese
who had settled in the East went into fishing or
farming or factory work. Particularly in New
England, workers for the textile mills were in high
demand. In California the Portuguese were out-

standing in dairy farming and in the raising of grapes for wine. Others went into fishing, fruit and vegetable farming, small businesses, and various crafts.

This forty-year period marks the height of Portuguese immigration to the United States; nearly 200,000 arrived and most settled where their fellow countrymen had settled before them. A 1920 report showed the following cities with the greatest number of Portuguese inhabitants: New Bedford, Massachusetts (17,000); Fall River, Massachusetts; Oakland, California; Providence, Rhode Island; Lowell, Massachusetts; Cambridge, Massachusetts; New York; and Boston (a little over 1,200).

Vascos Jardim, who arrived in 1920, described his first impressions of the United States:

> When I came from a small place and came to a big place, everything changed—not just freedom, because we had freedom in Portugal, too—but the development of the country, inventions, facilities. It's a nice life. Here you can do anything: go here, go there; and new things are coming out all the time. . . .
>
> I came by boat. I had no brothers or sisters or family in this country. . . . Suddenly I made up my mind, and said, "I'm going to America." I was not of age, and my father had to sign the passport. Well, I left Madeira Island, took a boat to the Azores, stayed in the Azores for three weeks, and from there came to the United States, landed in Providence, Rhode Island.[7]

Much of Vascos Jardim's early experience involved finding the right job so that he could support himself and succeed at something. After several jobs, Jardim moved to Newark, New Jersey, and founded a Portuguese-American newspaper, *Luso Americano*. The word *Luso* is related to *Lusitania,* the ancient name of the area roughly corresponding to modern Portugal. Still in existence, the paper covers events of interest to the Portuguese community. Jardim had found a way to succeed in America.

Jardim's case was unusual. A 1919 article in the *Literary Digest* described the work being done by most Portuguese-Americans:

> One half is settled in central California, the other in southeastern New England. The Portuguese in California are mainly engaged in agricultural pursuits and are conspicuous in that state as cultivators of vineyards for the wine industry. Many Portuguese raise fruits and other crops besides grapes and some also breed livestock and deal in dairy farm products. These men from Portugal own their farms and not a few are possessed of considerable wealth. As a class they are much more plentifully endowed with the world's goods than their compatriots in New England territory. . . .
>
> By far the greatest number of Portuguese in New England is employed in textile factories. In their native country they were farmers. The Portuguese colony at New Bedford, Massachu-

setts, traces its origin to a small number of natives from the Azores brought to these shores by New Bedford whalers. The fisheries of Cape Cod and Gloucester employ a sizable colony of Portuguese, while Portuguese from the Cape Verde Islands work in the cranberry bogs of Massachusetts. . . . Most of the Portuguese who come here come here to stay.[8]

The 1924 Immigration Act restricted Portuguese immigration to only 440 each year. This preceded by only a few years the fascist "new state" of Antonio de Oliveira Salazar, who became dictator in 1933. Repressive and cruel, the Salazar dictatorship subjugated the people for thirty-five years, keeping the country underdeveloped. It was one of the poorest in Europe and dependent on its African colonies of Angola, Portuguese Guinea, Mozambique, and the Cape Verde Islands.

The third major period of Portuguese immigration did not come until the 1950s, when nearly twenty thousand arrived in the United States. The new influx came largely as a result of a disastrous submarine volcanic eruption off the western end of the island of Fayal in the Azores. But Manuel Rosa arrived from mainland Portugal in 1956, when he was six. Coming from an isolated Portuguese village and not knowing the English language, six-year-old Manuel Rosa had a difficult time learning to get along with the other children in Newark, New Jersey:

My second experience in the United States was coming into a neighborhood of Newark at that time which was predominantly black, and I had never met black people in my life. . . . For the most part, it was a matter of survival. I used to run home every day. I had my share of beatings from them. I looked upon them with great hatred. Because we were the only whites on Cottage Street at the time, the only friends that I could play with were black children, and I used to come home crying every single day and my brothers and sisters and I were very much afraid. . . . As I gradually grew up, most of my friends were blacks, Puerto Ricans, Chinese, and Italians. I learned to live with them. I learned to play with them and eat with them and share things with them.[9]

Many of the Portuguese who settled in New Jersey in the 1950s became construction workers. Manuel Rosa said:

They take jobs where language and skill are not required, where a strong hard back is the most important thing to qualify for a job. What they knew in Portugal was hard work, and what they know here is hard work. Pick and shovel, that's what you get into. The women? They went into the garment industry for the most part. I'm talking about my time, 1956, when most of those who came over were from mainland Portugal.[10]

Rosa's father had a difficult time:

> He was working on the George Washington
> Bridge, building the second level. He remem-
> bers vividly that some of the men actually fell
> into one of the pillars that held up the George
> Washington Bridge. They actually fell into the
> concrete that was being poured. He worked for
> a number of construction companies and
> eventually he became disabled because of con-
> struction work. He had two heart attacks, and
> he was crippled with arthritis and rheumatism.
> He had an operation on his legs. He was in the
> construction industry eleven years and then
> he couldn't work any more. You have to
> understand that heavy construction is a
> rigorous profession. He was forty-six or forty-
> seven when he started, and it had its effect on
> him.
>
> If you're in that industry from the time
> you're twenty till forty-five, that's when it's
> time for you to go. You don't start when you're
> over forty and end at sixty. However, since
> there's no alternative, you must do that if you
> want to support a family of eleven people.[11]

Manuel Rosa and two of his brothers earned their
college degrees and now run their own real estate
agency in Newark. Manuel described the immigrants
who came after 1965, during the fourth wave, and
how different they are.

Those who are coming over here more recently are skilled people from Lisbon and other towns, and a lot of people from Angola, Mozambique, and other Portuguese colonies around the world. Now there are a number of technicians, skilled people such as carpenters, professional cooks, auto body repair people, mechanics, electricians, and plumbers. This was not known when we came here. You were a farmer—that's all that came over—knowing little of the language—but now we see a lot of people who are coming over here—they and their children already speak the English language, because teaching is fostered in Portugal now.[12]

The 1965 immigration law permitted unlimited admission of immediate relatives of United States citizens. During the 1960s Portuguese colonies began to revolt, and armed independence movements appeared in Angola, Mozambique, and Portuguese Guinea. The sending of Portuguese troops to suppress these insurrections started long and costly wars which drained the home economy. Ill and incapacitated, Salazar was succeeded by Marcello Caetano in 1968. Then, in 1974, Caetano was overthrown in a revolution led by liberal army officers seeking to end the African wars which were consuming the Portuguese budget and causing large numbers of citizens to emigrate. More than one hundred thousand came to America. Many of them, as in earlier times, came from the Azores, and many came to stay.

Even the most recent Portuguese immigrant, who probably will still choose to settle in one of the two great areas of Portuguese population in the United States, is carrying on a tradition that began long ago. No other people came earlier to the New World nor has another been there more continuously. Looking for a better life, the new immigrant has worked hard, like immigrants from other national groups, has met and dealt with strong feelings of prejudice against him or her, has partaken in new educational opportunities, and has contributed in many ways to American life. Such people as John Philip Sousa, "the March King"; John Dos Passos, the writer; and Tony Lema, golfer —all men of Portuguese descent—have brought pride to the Portuguese in particular and enriched American culture in general.

Meanwhile, in Portugal the struggle for modernization, diversity of capital and industry, and development of the country goes on. Democratic elections have been held, civil liberties have been restored, and independence for the African nations has come about. But until such time as the Portuguese people can find work and the possibility of a good life at home, many of them will continue to look for opportunities elsewhere through emigration.

FROM SPAIN

Chapter 9

The First to Settle

Many Spanish-speaking people have been coming to America from Puerto Rico, Mexico, Cuba, and other countries south of the borders of the United States, but we hardly ever hear about those who came directly from Spain, perhaps because there have been so few of them. In the history of recorded immigration, fewer than three hundred thousand immigrants have arrived from Spain, less than two percent of those who have come from all countries.

Spain is, however, directly responsible for the fact that an estimated twenty million people speak Spanish in the United States today. Dominating much of the Western Hemisphere, Spain was one of the most powerful countries in the world during the sixteenth century. At one time Spain controlled Florida, Louisiana, Texas, California, New Mexico, and all the western Great Plains—not to mention large parts of Central and South America and the Caribbean. However, Spain was primarily interested in the New World as a source of riches, not as an area to colonize. Spanish citizens were not encouraged to settle in the New World, though Balboa, Ponce de León, De Soto, and Coronado led exploratory expeditions along both coasts and claimed large portions of the Southwest for Spain.

Nonetheless, Spanish settlers founded a colony in Pensacola, Florida, in 1559. It failed, but another colony, founded in 1565 at St. Augustine, prospered. It was the first permanent European community in North America, and when the New Smyrna colony failed in 1777, the residents found a haven in St. Augustine. Some of these had come from Minorca, an island in the Mediterranean. Their influence and family names (such as Pomar, Benet, Andreu, Capo, Pertall, Segui) may still be found in St. Augustine today.

Spanish soldiers—*conquistadores*—seeking the legendary Seven Cities of Cíbola, where the streets were said to be paved with gold, founded Santa Fe, New Mexico, in 1610. In the eighteenth century Franciscan missionaries, encouraged by the Spanish government, established missions all along the California coast, most notably the one at San Francisco in 1776.

Still, by 1781 there were only six hundred Spaniards living in California and not many more in the other territories they controlled. With the acquisition of the Louisiana territory from France in 1762, the Spaniards were in control of the land from Florida to California. But soon after, the Florida territory was ceded to the British, and in

1800 the Louisiana territory was returned to the French (who in turn sold it to the young United States in 1803). Later the Spanish regained Florida, only to lose it, as well as Mexico, in 1821 in the war for Mexican independence.

So the Florida and California Spaniards faded as an ethnic group. They left behind many place names. Eight states have Spanish names—Florida, California, Nevada, Colorado, New Mexico, Arizona, Texas, and Montana—as do many cities— San Francisco, Los Angeles, San Antonio, La Jolla, San José. They also left behind Spanish colonial architecture and the beginnings of a new culture that would have genuine survival and durability in the Hispanic Southwest.[1]

Today this Hispanic culture has spread, fed by the influx of immigrants from Latin America, including Puerto Rico. It is estimated that only four cities in the world have a larger Spanish-speaking population than New York—Madrid, Mexico City, Barcelona, and Buenos Aires.

In more recent times the greatest wave of "new immigration" from southern and eastern Europe brought some people from Spain. From 1900 to 1924, over 174,000 arrived, but some 72,000 of them returned home. Millions of Spaniards emigrated at that time from Spain, but most of them went to South and Central America, primarily to Argentina and Cuba, where they knew they would encounter no language barrier.

The majority of those who came to the United States emigrated because they were unable to earn a living in Spain. In southern Spain there were more agricultural workers than could find jobs on the large estates. In Galicia, a province of northern Spain, the *minifundio,* a system for dividing land among relatives, led to smaller and smaller plots of land until they became too small for a family to cultivate. Sometimes a person would inherit a piece of land as small as four feet square. Some heard from successful relatives already in America. Many who emigrated earlier returned to Spain after they had saved enough money to live in comfort. This encouraged others to try their luck in America. The agents of steamship lines also spread the word about the riches to be had in the United States.

The big stumbling block to the trip was money. Many families underwent great hardships repaying loans at exorbitant interest rates in order to pay for the journey in overcrowded, unsanitary ship steerage. There were many illnesses and deaths before those ships reached these shores. When the immigrants arrived, many suffered unemployment and loneliness.

As with other immigrants from southern Europe, the men from Spain outnumbered the women during the peak years of immigration. The men saved money and returned to Spain or settled down and sent for the families. Some went back and returned with Spanish wives.

Most of the immigrants from Spain came from Galicia and the Basque regions in northern Spain and settled in New York City and vicinity. They established their own newspapers, like *La Prensa,* a widely distributed Spanish-language newspaper, and set up self-help organizations like Casa Galicia and the Centro Vasco (Basque) Americano.

Other Spanish immigrants came to the United States from Andalusia, in the southwestern corner of Spain. Agents of the Hawaii Sugar Planters Association arranged for their passage and for jobs on Hawaiian plantations. Most came on six shiploads during the years 1907, 1911, 1912, and 1913. But by 1920 almost all of these workers had moved to California, where they either settled in the cities or found work on the fruit farms. Once they had formed settlements, others joined them directly from Andalusia.

Florida has long been a center of Spanish settlement. Most of those who came in the "new immigration" from Spain were originally Asturian cigar makers who went to Key West and Tampa by way of Cuba. Other Spanish immigrants went to live and work in the industrial centers of Illinois, Michigan, Ohio, and Pennsylvania, and in the coal mining towns of West Virginia.

The Basques live partly in Spain and partly in France, and speak a language of mysterious origin. They came in large numbers during the first two decades of this century from the four Basque provinces on the Bay of Biscay at the western end of the Pyrenees Mountains in northern Spain, just south of France. For hundreds of years Basques have been herding sheep on the steep hills and deep valleys of the Pyrenees. They have continued this vocation in the Rocky Mountains. The city of Boise, located in the center of the Idaho-Nevada sheep ranges, has become known as the Basque capital of the United States. During the 1950s special immigration laws were passed to allow Basque sheepherders to enter the United States on nonquota visas when the supply of sheepherders became short.

San Francisco became an important recreational center for Basques from many states. They are known for their adherence to their distinctive language and customs, for their independent spirit and achievement through hard work. Julia Cooley Altrocchi, described some Basque sheepherders and their lives in California in a 1938 magazine article:

> Even in their simple, Americanized clothes, the Basques seem to have a feeling for the picturesque and for the consonances of color. Mr. Yanci wore blue overalls, a blue shirt, a blue sweater and a white green-spotted cap. The jaunty Basque beret had been discarded. "They wear the beret when they come—and when they die. *They insist on being buried in it,*" a neighbor told us later. "They dress American after they get here."
>
> Nate Yanci leaned over his fence and talked reluctantly, with long seas of silence between the sails of his words.
>
> "Sheep going well?" we asked.
>
> "I try." (Noncommittally as a New Englander).
>
> "It's pretty here."

"Yes. So pretty as anywhere. Almost so pretty as Spain. Hills not so high."

"You come from the Spanish Basque country?"

"Navarra."

"Have you been here long?"

"Been here in California fourteen years. In America thirty years."

"Have you many sheep?"

"Fifteen hundred sheep. Rent twelve hundred acres of land."

"Are there many Basques around here?"

"Yes. Some Basques. It good here. Some *make America*."

This phrase, "make America," interested us greatly, for it is precisely the phrase that the Italian immigrant, who makes money, is successful, uses. He also "makes America"!

"Do they go back after they make America?" we asked. Noncommittally again came the answer:

"I don't know. Might as well stay where make the living."[2]

The Basques maintained their customs and tradition in the Rocky Mountains. Relating a conversation with another Basque family, Altrocchi wrote:

In the course of my questionings, I learned that, like many other Basques, on New Year's Eve and at Epiphany, Mr. La Cabe goes from Basque house to Basque house, singing old folk songs. But it was the word "dance" which made Mrs. La Cabe's face suddenly luminous.

"Oh, yes," she said, "I always dance the *jota* at the dancing parties. I love it!—And if I have no castanets, I snap the music with my fingers!"[3]

The author went on:

In San Francisco itself, there are little islands of Basques. There is even a *Salon de Pelota,* or *Juego de Pelota,* on Pacific Avenue, that is, a courtyard constructed for the playing of the great old Basque game of *pelota* (or *jai alai*), a very old game of ball in which the hand is used like a tennis racket. . . . There are two small hotels, which cater almost entirely to Basques, the Hotel Español and the Hotel de España, "Headquarters for Wool Sheep Cattlemen," on Broadway.[4]

Immigration from Spain virtually stopped after 1924, when the quota system went into effect. For years, only 252 Spaniards were allowed to enter the United States each year.

From 1931 to 1936 Spain was a democratic republic for the first time in its history. But the world was in a deep economic depression, and Spain was poorer than ever. Socialist, Communist, anarchist, and trade union groups found the government reforms too moderate. The Church and the army resisted the government's attempts to limit their power. The country was deeply split between leftist and rightist factions in every sphere of life, and the government was not able to control strikes and violence in the streets.

In 1936 the army finally mutinied, and civil war began. The rebels, who called themselves Nationalists, were led by General Francisco Franco. They had the support of the conservative groups of the Catholic Church, the middle class, and the land-owning peasants, as well as the Falange—the Spanish fascist movement—and the backers of the exiled king. The Republican side, known as the Loyalists, was backed by the workers, the liberals, Socialists, Communists, anarchists, and the Separatists, such as the Basques and the Catalonians.

The Basques actually enjoyed independence for a brief period, and they strongly resisted the Franco insurgents. Even in faraway California, a Basque woman from Navarra expressed her feelings:

> "Yes, my father is there. My relatives are there. We write and receive no answer. Many of our young men went over to get Spanish wives and have remained in Spain to fight. Yes, we are all Loyalists."[5]

The Basque town of Guernica became a symbol of both Basque and Loyalist repression when it was destroyed in 1937 by German planes sent to aid Franco. Seen by Hitler and Mussolini as a rehearsal for World War II, the Spanish civil war provided a proving grounds for new planes and weapons, and the large-scale bombing of civilians began for the first time. The famous painting depicting the agony of Guernica by the Spanish artist Pablo Picasso has hung in the Museum of Modern Art in New York City since the civil war, on loan from the artist. Picasso specified that it be sent to Spain only when the country had a republican form of government. At this writing, the date of the painting's departure for Spain is still uncertain.

The end of the bloody war came in 1939 with Franco as victor. Casualties may have been as high as one million; many people were imprisoned; and at least 250,000 Spaniards fled the country, mainly across the French border. Only a few made their way to the United States.

The American government had denied aid to the Republican forces and excluded Spanish exiles even after the United States entered World War II, pledged to end fascism. The socialist and anarchist leanings of the Loyalists were sources of anxiety to the U.S. government, which had a long history of opposing "foreign radicals." Going back to the Alien and Sedition Acts of 1789 and including the period following the Russian Revolution and World War I, Congress passed antianarchist and anti-Communist laws in 1918 and 1920, and detained and deported alien dissidents. The fear of foreign radicals was to outlive World War II and continue into the McCarthy era of the 1950s, as the experiences of "Andres Aragon," a pseudonym, show.

Aragon was one of the very few Spaniards who came to America. Educated at the University of Granada, Aragon became involved in the Republican struggle and eventually had to flee Spain. He was able to make his way to Cuba, and in 1943 he came to the United States as a result of the intervention of a professor at Princeton University, where Aragon taught briefly. He later worked for the Department of War Information, but was fired when he refused to translate a pro-Franco speech for rebroadcast to Spain. For a while he worked with the Spanish movie director, Luis Buñuel, who was then in America. When Buñuel went to Mexico, Aragon could not follow him because of his immigration status.

Eventually, Aragon got a job teaching at a university in Los Angeles. The Immigration authorities told him he could go to Canada to get a reentry visa for permanent residency in the United States. In the meantime, he was declared a Communist—he was not—by the House Un-American Activities Committee in Washington. Arrested in Canada, he was sent to jail in Seattle, and ordered deported. It was 1955. It was to take another year, and the intervention of the chancellor of the university, who had influential relatives in Washington, for Aragon finally to become a citizen.

June Namias, who interviewed Aragon and wrote up his story for her book *First Generation: In the Words of Twentieth-Century American Immigrants*,[6] said to him: "I'm surprised you would want to become a citizen after all that."

Aragon replied:

After so many years of living in the United States I can't judge the authorities on the same

level with the American people. I had excellent
American friends, I worked in excellent
libraries, I was able to do what I wanted to do
with my life. I liked American people in
general. I felt at ease here, and I think I am
now convinced that the only country that I
like to live in and die in is the United States,
in spite of all these experiences. If I remember
these anecdotes, it is because they were
dramatic, but everybody goes in life through
bad experiences and bad things and I had my
share, probably more than other people. I
accepted and I wanted American citizenship,
and I feel very comfortable being American.
But it's good for other people to know that
these things happen in a democracy, too, and
[not only under totalitarian rule]. Perhaps
other people may think I have a right to be
bitter. I am not bitter at all.

I went back to Spain for the first time after
twenty years. I saw my parents one year before
they died. I went back several times for short
visits. It is hard for me to understand the
people.

My family stayed, my brother and sister,
and it was hard for me to talk to them. I found
that the psychology of the people is very much
changed, the character of the people. It is not
the people I knew as Spaniards, and it is no
wonder. They lived through such terrible times
—and human beings, they get accustomed to
everything. If you are forced to live like that,

it becomes a habit. To change all of a sudden, it is not easy. That country under Franco made me sick. I felt much closer to the American people than that type of life, and I would never go back to live under any type of lack of freedom, lack of dignity.

Since the death of Franco in 1975, King Juan Carlos has become head of state. Already well on the way to industrialization, Spain is now slowly coming to grips with the problems of modern life and is trying to deal with all the forces pushing for full democratic existence—including the Basques who are still pushing for independence—as well as seeking closer ties with Europe. As in Portugal, the years of suppressed freedom have taken their toll, and only time will tell how the institutions bequeathed by dictatorship will survive or change.

After the U.S. Immigration Act of 1965 lifted the quota system, large numbers of Spaniards again applied for immigration, many no doubt to escape the Franco regime, then still in power. Whether or not they will still want to come in the future remains to be seen.

Notes

Introduction

1. Quoted in Willard A. Heaps, *The Story of Ellis Island* (New York: Seabury Press, 1967), p. 19.
2. Ibid., p. 60.
3. Ibid., p. 69.
4. Interview with Anastasia Stephanios, in *They Chose America: Conversations with Immigrants*, Vol. 2, An Audio Cassette Program (Princeton, N.J.: Visual Education Corp., 1975).
5. Quoted in Richard Gambino, *Blood of My Blood* (Garden City, N.Y.: Doubleday & Co., 1974), p. 255.
6. Ibid., p. 71.
7. Quoted in Bernard A. Weisberger, *The American Heritage History of the American People* (New York: American Heritage Publishing Co., 1971), p. 251.
8. Quoted in Gambino, *Blood of My Blood,* pp. 72–73.

9. Ibid., pp. 109–10.
10. Quoted in Weisberger, *American Heritage History,* p. 253.

FROM ITALY

Chapter 1.   Leaving Home

1. Alexander DeConde, *Half Bitter, Half Sweet: An Excursion into Italian-American History* (New York: Charles Scribner's Sons, 1971), p. 1.
2. Quoted in Wayne Moquin and Charles Van Doren eds., *A Documentary History of the Italian Americans* (New York: Praeger Publishers, 1975), p. 32.
3. Constantine M. Panunzio, *The Soul of an Immigrant* (1921; reprint ed., New York: Arno Press and New York Times, 1969), pp. 59–60.
4. Salvatore Saladino, *Italy from Unification to 1919* (New York: Thomas Y. Crowell Co., 1970), p. 20.
5. Interview with Vincent Gianelli, in *They Chose America,* Vol. 1.
6. Interview with Clarence Silva, in *They Chose America,* Vol. 1.
7. Pascal D'Angelo, *Son of Italy* (New York: Arno Press, 1975), pp. 1–3.
8. Rocco Corresca, "The Biography of a Bootblack," in John Appel, ed., *The New Immigration* (New York: Pitman Publishing Corp., 1971), pp. 56–57.
9. Heaps, *Ellis Island,* pp. 36–37.
10. Ibid., pp. 41–42.

Chapter 2. Finding Work

1. Panunzio, *Soul of an Immigrant,* pp. 75–77.
2. Quoted in DeConde, *Half Bitter, Half Sweet,* p. 86.
3. Gambino, *Blood of My Blood,* p. 71.
4. D'Angelo, *Son of Italy,* p. 115.
5. Quoted in Moquin and Van Doren, *History of Italian Americans,* p. 103.
6. Panunzio, *Soul of an Immigrant,* pp. 110–11.
7. Ibid., pp. 114–15.
8. Ibid., p. 129.
9. Ibid., p. 140.

Chapter 3. New Horizons

1. Quoted in Andrew F. Rolle, *The American Italians: Their History and Culture* (Belmont, Calif.: Wadsworth Publishing Co., 1972), pp. 73–74.
2. Quoted in Moquin and Van Doren, *History of Italian Americans,* p. 115.
3. Ibid., p. 156.
4. Quoted in Gambino, *Blood of My Blood,* p. 92.
5. Quoted in Luciano J. Iorizzo and Salvatore Mondello, *The Italian-Americans* (New York: Twayne Publishers, 1971), p. 116.
6. Ibid., p. 131.
7. Ibid., p. 69.
8. Jacob A. Riis, *How the Other Half Lives: Studies Among the Tenements of New York* (New York: Hill and Wang, 1957), pp. 48–49.
9. Ibid., p. 51.
10. Quoted in Valentine Rossilli Winsey, "The Italian Immigrant Women Who Arrived in the United States Before World War I," in Francesco

Cordasco, ed., *Studies in Italian American Social History* (Totowa, N.J.: Rowman and Littlefield, 1975), p. 201.

11. Panunzio, *Soul of an Immigrant,* p. 228.
12. Ibid., p. 241.
13. Moquin and Van Doren, *History of Italian Americans,* pp. 314–15.
14. Ibid., p. 315.

Chapter 4. Settling In

1. Panunzio, *Soul of an Immigrant,* pp. 254–55.
2. Quoted in Francesco Cordasco and Eugene Bucchioni, eds., *The Italians: Social Backgrounds of an American Group* (Clifton, N.J.: Augustus M. Kelley Publishers, 1974), p. 528.
3. Quoted in Weisberger, *American Heritage History,* p. 369.
4. Panunzio, *Soul of an Immigrant,* pp. 149–50.
5. Ibid., pp. 164–65.
6. Quoted in Erik Amfitheatrof, *The Children of Columbus: An Informal History of the Italians in the New World* (Boston: Little, Brown & Co., 1973), pp. 187–88.
7. Ibid., p. 233.
8. Moquin and Van Doren, *History of Italian Americans,* p. 193.
9. Quoted in Wayne Moquin, ed., *Makers of America,* Vol. 9, *Refugees and Victims 1939–1954* (Chicago: Encyclopedia Britannica Educational Corp., 1971), pp. 11–12.
10. Quoted in Moquin, *Makers of America,* Vol. 9, pp. 36–38.
11. Panunzio, *Soul of an Immigrant,* pp. 311–12.
12. Ibid., pp. 324–25.

FROM GREECE

Chapter 5.   The Decision to Leave
1. "Life Story of a Pushcart Peddlar," *The Independent,* Vol. 60 (1960), p. 274.
2. Quoted in Theodore Saloutos, *The Greeks in the United States* (Cambridge: Harvard University Press, 1964), p. 30.
3. Ibid., p. 32.
4. Quoted in Theodore Saloutos, *They Remember America: The Story of the Repatriated Greek-Americans* (Berkeley: University of California Press, 1956), p. 3.
5. Interview with Achilles Manolakis, in *They Chose America,* Vol. 2.
6. Interview with George Kokkas, in *They Chose America,* Vol. 2.

Chapter 6.   Making a Living
1. Interview with Sam Fortosis, in *They Chose America,* Vol. 2.
2. Quoted in Saloutos, *They Remember America,* p. 10.
3. Quoted in Leola Benedict Terhune, "The Greek Bootblack," *The Survey,* Vol. 26 (September 16, 1911), pp. 853–54.
4. Quoted in Saloutos, *Greeks in the United States,* p. 55.
5. Saloutos, *They Remember America,* p. 15.
6. Quoted in Edith Abbott, *Immigration: Select Documents and Case Records* (Chicago: University of Chicago Press, 1924), pp. 530–31.
7. Quoted in Saloutos, *They Remember America,* p. 7.

8. Interview with George Vordakis, in *They Chose America,* Vol. 2.

Chapter 7. Settling In

1. Quoted in Moquin, *Makers of America,* Vol. 6, *The New Immigrants 1904–1913,* pp. 52–53.
2. Interview with Sam Fortosis, in *They Chose America,* Vol. 2.
3. Quoted in Saloutos, *They Remember America,* p. 41.
4. Ibid., p. 41.
5. Ibid., p. 47.
6. Ibid., p. 47.
7. Ibid., p. 47.
8. Interview with Anastasia Stephanios, in *They Chose America,* Vol. 2.
9. J.P. Xenides, *The Greeks in America* (New York: George H. Doran Co., 1922), p. 88.
10. Demitra Georgas, *Greek Settlement in the San Francisco Bay Area,* reprint of a thesis, University of California, 1951 (San Francisco: R and E Research Assoc., 1974), p. 41.
11. Quoted in Saloutos, *Greeks in the United States,* pp. 88–89.
12. Ibid., p. 72.
13. Moquin, *Makers of America,* Vol. 8, *Children of the Melting Pot 1925–1938,* pp. 133–34.
14. Ariadne Thompson, *The Octagonal Heart* (Indianapolis and New York: Bobbs-Merrill Co., 1956), pp. 68–69.
15. Interview with Achilles Manolakis, in *They Chose America,* Vol. 2.
16. Ibid.

FROM PORTUGAL

Chapter 8.   A Long Tradition

1. John B. Edlefsen, "Portuguese Americans," in Francis J. Brown and Joseph S. Roucek, eds., *One America,* 3rd ed. (Englewood Cliffs, N.J.: Prentice-Hall, 1952), p. 262. Also, Manoel daSilveira Cardozo, comp. and ed., *The Portuguese in America, 590 B.C.–1974* (Dobbs Ferry, N.Y.: Oceana Publications, 1976), p. 5.
2. Quoted in Abraham J. Karp, ed., *Golden Door to America: The Jewish Immigrant Experience* (New York: Viking Press, 1976), p. 21.
3. Ibid., p. 22.
4. Ibid., p. 23.
5. Quoted in Cardoza, *Portuguese in America,* p. 45.
6. Quoted in Moquin, *Makers of America,* Vol. 7, *Hyphenated Americans 1914–1924,* pp. 186–87.
7. Interview with Vascos Jardim by Gladys Nadler Rips, Newark, N.J. (April 13, 1978).
8. "Portuguese in America," *Literary Digest,* Vol. 63 (November 22, 1919), p. 40.
9. Interview with Manuel Rosa by Gladys Nadler Rips, Newark, N.J. (April 13, 1978).
10. Ibid.
11. Ibid.
12. Ibid.

FROM SPAIN

Chapter 9.   The First to Settle

1. Wilbur Zelinsky, *The Cultural Geography of the United States* (Englewood Cliffs, N.J.: Prentice-Hall, 1973), p. 27.
2. Julia Cooley Altrocchi, "The Spanish Basques in

California," *The Catholic World,* Vol. 146, No.
874 (January 1938), p. 420.
3. Ibid., p. 422.
4. Ibid., p. 423.
5. Ibid., p. 419.
6. June Namias, *First Generation: In the Words
   of Twentieth-Century American Immigrants*
   (Boston: Beacon Press, 1978), pp. 99–109.

Suggested Reading

Abbott, Edith. *Immigration: Select Documents and Case Records.* Chicago: University of Chicago Press, 1924.

Amfitheatrof, Erik. *The Children of Columbus: An Informal History of the Italians in the New World.* Boston: Little, Brown & Co., 1973.

Appel, John, ed. *The New Immigration.* New York: Pitman, 1971.

Barzini, Luigi. *The Italians.* New York: Atheneum, 1964.

Brown, Francis J., and Joseph S. Roucek, eds. *One America: The History, Contributions, and Present Problems of Our Racial Minorities.* 3rd ed. Englewood Cliffs, N.J.: Prentice-Hall, 1952.

Cardozo, Manoel daSilveira, comp. and ed. *The Portuguese in America 590 B.C.–1974.* Dobbs Ferry, N.Y.: Oceana Publications, 1976.

Coppa, Frank J., and Thomas J. Curran. *The Immi-*

grant *Experience in America.* Boston: Twayne Publishers, 1976. (See: "The Hispanic Impact Upon the United States" by Theodore S. Beardsley, Jr.)

Cordasco, Francesco, ed. *Studies in Italian American Social History.* Totowa, N.J.: Rowman and Littlefield, 1975.

————, and Eugene Bucchioni, eds. *The Italians: Social Backgrounds of an American Group.* Clifton, N.J.: Augustus M. Kelley Publishers, 1974.

Corsi, Edward. *In the Shadow of Liberty.* 1935. Reprint. New York: Arno Press and New York Times, 1969.

D'Angelo, Pascal. *Son of Italy.* New York: Arno Press, 1975.

DeConde, Alexander. *Half Bitter, Half Sweet: An Excursion into Italian-American History.* New York: Charles Scribner's Sons, 1971.

Dos Passos, John, *The Portugal Story: Three Centuries of Exploration and Discovery.* New York: Doubleday & Co., 1969.

Fenton, Heike, and Melvin Hecker. *The Greeks in America 1528–1977.* Dobbs Ferry, N.Y.: Oceana Publications, 1978.

Gambino, Richard. *Blood of My Blood.* Garden City, N.Y.: Doubleday & Co., 1974.

Georgas, Demitra. *Greek Settlement in the San Francisco Bay Area.* Reprint. Thesis, University of California, 1951. San Francisco: R and E Research Assoc., 1974.

Heaps, Willard A. *The Story of Ellis Island.* New York: Seabury Press, 1967.

134 *Suggested Reading*

Holden, David. *Greece Without Columns: The Making of Modern Greece.* Philadelphia: J.B. Lippincott Co., 1972.

Iorizzo, Luciano, and Salvatore Mondello. *The Italian-Americans.* Boston: Twayne Publishers, 1971.

Karp, Abraham J. *Golden Door to America: The Jewish Immigrant Experience.* New York: Viking Press, 1976.

Livermore, H.V. *A Short History of Portugal.* Chicago: Aldine Publishing Co., 1973.

Maas, Peter. *The Valachi Papers.* New York: G.P. Putnam's Sons, 1968.

McGovern, (Senator) George. *Revolution into Democracy: Portugal After the Coup.* Report to the Committee on Foreign Relations, United States Senate. Washington: U.S. Government Printing Office, 1976.

Moquin, Wayne, ed. *Makers of America.* 10 vols. Chicago: Encyclopedia Britannica Educational Corp., 1971.

————, and Charles Van Doren, eds. *A Documentary History of the Italian Americans.* New York: Praeger Publishers, 1975.

Namias, June. *First Generation: In the Words of Twentieth-Century American Immigrants.* Boston: Beacon Press, 1978.

Natella, Arthur A. comp. and ed. *The Spanish in America 1513–1974.* Dobbs Ferry, N.Y.: Oceana Publications, 1975.

Panunzio, Constantine M. *The Soul of an Immigrant.* 1921. Reprint. New York: Arno Press and New York Times, 1969.

Riis, Jacob A. *How the Other Half Lives: Studies*

Among the Tenements of New York. New York: Hill and Wang, 1957.

Rolle, Andrew F. *The American Italians: Their History and Culture.* Belmont, Calif.: Wadsworth Publishing Co., 1972.

Saladino, Salvatore. *Italy from Unification to 1919.* New York: Thomas Y. Crowell Co., 1970.

Saloutos, Theodore. *The Greeks in the United States.* Cambridge: Harvard University Press, 1964.

————. *They Remember America: The Story of the Repatriated Greek-Americans.* Berkeley: University of California Press, 1956.

Salvadori, Massimo. *Italy.* Englewood Cliffs, N.J.: Prentice-Hall, 1965.

Salvatorelli, Luigi. *The Risorgimento: Thought and Action.* Trans. Mario Domandi. New York: Harper and Row, 1970.

Smith, Denis Mack. *Italy: A Modern History.* Ann Arbor: University of Michigan Press, 1969.

Thomas, Hugh. *The Spanish Civil War.* Rev. and enl. ed. New York: Harper and Row, 1977.

Thompson, Ariadne. *The Octagonal Heart.* Indianapolis and New York: Bobbs-Merrill Co., 1956.

Trevelyan, J.P. *A Short History of the Italian People: From the Barbarian Invasions to the Present Day.* New York: Pitman Publishing Corp. 1956.

Tuohy, Frank, and Graham Finlayson. *Portugal.* New York: Viking Press, 1970.

Weisberger, Bernard A. *The American Heritage History of the American People.* New York: American Heritage Publishing Co., 1971.

Wittke, Carl. *We Who Built America: The Saga of the Immigrant.* Englewood Cliffs, N.J.: Prentice-Hall, 1939.

Woodhouse, C.M. *A Short History of Modern Greece.* New York: Praeger Publishers, 1968.

Xenides, J.P., *The Greeks in America.* New York: George H. Doran Co., 1922.

Zelinsky, Wilbur. *The Cultural Geography of the United States.* Englewood Cliffs, N.J.: Prentice-Hall, 1973.

A Brief History of U.S. Immigration Laws

The authority to formulate immigration policy rests with Congress and is contained in Article 1, Section 8, Clause 3 of the Constitution, which provides that Congress shall have the power to "regulate commerce with foreign nations, and among the several States, and with the Indian tribes."

Alien Act of 1798: authorized the deportation of aliens by the President. Expired after two years.

For the next seventy-five years there was no federal legislation restricting admission to, or allowing deportation from, the United States.

Act of 1875: excluded criminals and prostitutes and entrusted inspection of immigrants to collectors of the ports.

Act of 1882: excluded lunatics and idiots and persons liable to becoming a public charge.

First Chinese Exclusion Act.

Acts of 1885 and 1887: contract labor laws, which made it unlawful to import aliens under contract for labor or services of any kind. (Exceptions: artists, lecturers, servants, skilled aliens in an industry not yet established in the United States, etc.).

Act of 1888: amended previous acts to provide for expulsion of aliens landing in violation of contract laws.

Act of 1891: first exclusion of persons with certain diseases; felons, also persons having committed crimes involving moral turpitude; polygamists, etc.

Act of 1903: further exclusion of persons with certain mental diseases, epilepsy, etc.; beggars; also "anarchists or persons who believe in, or advocate the overthrow by force or violence of the Government of the United States or of all government or of all forms of law or the assassination of public officials." Further refined deportation laws.

Acts of 1907, 1908: further exclusions for health reasons, such as TB.

Exclusion of persons detrimental to labor conditions in the United States, specifically Japanese and Korean skilled or unskilled laborers.

Gentlemen's Agreement with Japan: in which Japan agreed to restrictions imposed by the United States.

Act of 1917: codified previous exclusion provisions, and added literacy test. Further restricted entry of other Asians.

Act of 1921: First Quota Law, in which approximately 350,000 immigrants were permitted entry, mostly from northern or western Europe.

Act of 1924: National Origins Quota System set annual limitations on the number of aliens of any nationality immigrating to the United States. The act also decreed, in a provision aimed primarily at the Japanese, that no aliens ineligible to citizenship could be admitted to the United States.

"Gigolo Act" of 1937: allowing deportation of aliens fraudulently marrying in order to enter the United States either by having marriage annulled or by refusing to marry once having entered the country.

Act of 1940: Alien Registration Act provided for registration and fingerprinting of all aliens.

Act of 1943: Chinese Exclusion Acts repealed.

Act of 1945: War Brides Act admitted during the three years of act's existence approximately 118,000 brides, grooms, and children of servicemen who had married foreign nationals during World War II.

Act of 1949: Displaced Persons Act admitted more than four hundred thousand people displaced as a result of World War II (to 1952).

Act of 1950: Internal Security Act excluded from immigrating any present or foreign member of the Communist party, and made more easily deportable people of this class already in the United States. Also provided for alien registration by January 10 of each year.

Act of 1952: Immigration and Nationality Act codified all existing legislation; also eliminated race as a bar to immigration.

Acts of 1953–1956: Refugee Relief acts admitted orphans, Hungarians after 1956 uprising, skilled sheepherders.

1957: special legislation to admit Hungarian refugees.

1960: special legislation paroled Cuban refugees into the United States.

Act of 1965: legislation amending act of 1952 phased out national origins by 1968, with new numerical ceilings on a first come, first served basis. Numerical ceilings (per annum): 120,000 for natives of the Western Hemisphere; 170,000 for natives of the Eastern Hemisphere. New preference categories: relatives (74 percent), scientists, artists (1 percent), skilled and unskilled labor (10 percent), refugees (6 percent).

Act of 1977: allowed Indochinese who had been paroled into the United States to adjust their status to permanent resident.

1979: Presidential directive allowed thousands of Vietnamese "boat people" to enter the United States.

Index